Reviving the Rails

Examining America's
Passenger Train Future

Peter Wretzky

Table of Contents

Introduction   1
The Golden Age of American Passenger   5
Rail
    Introduction to Early Rail Pioneers   6
    Impact of Transcontinental Railroads   10
    on Westward Expansion
    Technological Innovations in the   13
    Railway Sector
    Cultural Significance of Rail Travel in   17
    America
    Economic Contributions During the   20
    Late 19th and Early 20th Centuries
    Summary and Reflections   23
The Downfall Begins: Post-War Decline   25
    Rise of Automobile Culture   26
    Expansion of the Interstate Highway   30
    System
    Competition from the Airline   35
    Industry
    Declining Investments in Rail   39
    Infrastructure
    Union Strikes and Labor Issues   41
    Summary and Reflections   46
Trying to Stay Afloat: The 1960s and   47
70s
    Government Policy Shifts   48
    Formation of Amtrak   52
    Cutbacks and Service Reductions   56
    Public Perception Issues   61
    Notable Failures and Limited   64
    Successes
    Final Thoughts   67
Challenges Faced by Amtrak   69
    Budget Constraints   70

Maintenance and Aging Infrastructure 72

Service Reliability Problems 76

Political Influences and Funding Issues 80

Customer Satisfaction and Service Quality 84

Final Thoughts 86

Routes That Work: Success Stories 88

Northeast Corridor 89

California's Pacific Surfliner 91

Chicago-based Regional Services 95

Emerging High-Speed Rail Projects 98

Factors Contributing to Their Success 102

Final Thoughts 105

International Case Study: Japan's Shinkansen 107

Historical Background 108

Technological Advancements 112

Operational Efficiency 116

Economic Impacts 120

Cultural Acceptance and Popularity 123

Final Insights 126

European Excellence: High-Speed Networks 128

France's TGV 129

Germany's ICE 131

Spain's AVE 135

Cross-border interoperability 138

Funding models and government support 142

Final Insights 145

Environmental Benefits of Rail Travel 147

Reducing Carbon Emissions 148

Energy Efficiency Comparisons 152

Urban Congestion Alleviation 156

Land Use and Conservation 160
Rail Transport in Climate Change 163
Mitigation Policies
Final Insights 167
Economic Impacts of Revitalizing 169
Passenger Rail
Job Creation and Economic Stimulus 170
Economic Impacts of Revitalizing 170
Passenger Rail
Boosting Local Economies Along Rail 173
Corridors
Increase in Tourism and Mobility 177
Cost-Benefit Analysis of Rail 181
Investment
Long-Term Economic Sustainability 185
Final Thoughts 189
Technological Innovations and Future 191
Trends
Maglev Technology 192
Automation and AI in Rail Operations 196
Hyperloop Concepts 199
Advances in Track and Infrastructure 201
Materials
Digital Ticketing and Customer 206
Experience Improvements
Bringing It All Together 210
Policy and Legislative Frameworks 212
Federal vs State Responsibilities 213
Funding and Grants 217
Regulatory Hurdles 221
Public-Private Partnerships (PPPs) 225
Incentives for Rail Development 229
Summary and Reflections 234
Overcoming Societal Resistance 236
Changing Public Perceptions 237

Community Engagement and Participation   241

Addressing Concerns of Rural Areas   244

Marketing and Advocacy Strategies   249

Overcoming Societal Resistance   249

The Role of Media in Shaping Opinions   254

Concluding Thoughts   258

Regional and Local Initiatives   260

State-level rail projects   261

Inter-city rail connections   265

Light rail and commuter trains   267

Integration with other public transport modes   271

Unique solutions for different regions   275

Final Thoughts   278

Lessons from Failed Projects   280

California High-Speed Rail Challenges   281

Florida's Failed Initiatives   284

Mismanagement and Corruption Cases   288

Public Opposition Case Studies   292

Adaptation of Failure into Learning Experiences   295

Bringing It All Together   299

Vision for the Future   301

Blueprint for a National High-Speed Rail Network   302

Investment Priorities   306

Collaborative Governance Models   310

Emphasis on Sustainable Practices   315

Engagement and Education for the Public   318

Summary and Reflections   322

Conclusion   324

References

Chapter One

Introduction

I n the late 19th century, a journey across America by train was not just a means of travel but a symbol of progress. Imagine the thrill of passengers as they boarded luxurious coaches with elegant dining cars, charts in hand, eager to traverse the vast landscapes that define the essence of a young nation. The railroads served as the arteries of a growing country, connecting distant cities and small towns, driving economic growth and making it possible for people to travel in ways they had never imagined before.

We begin our story in this golden age of American passenger rail, an era that encapsulates so much of what rail travel represented: innovation, connection, and sheer adventure. Trains were more than just mechanical marvels; they embodied hope and opportunity, a technological leap forward that promised endless possibilities. Yet, just as the whistle of the train signaled hope, the mid-20th century ushered in a somber reality. The 1950s brought dramatic changes, and the clatter of wheels on steel gradually faded, replaced by the roar of engines on new highways. Personal automobiles became king, offering a new type of freedom and convenience that the railroads struggled to match. As the allure of car ownership grew, railroads found themselves battling decline, trying to adapt to an era that increasingly favored asphalt over iron rails.

The rapid transformation from the heyday of rail to its subsequent decline invites us to ask some tough questions. How did we transition so swiftly away from a mode of transport that once captured America's imagination? And perhaps more importantly, why should we care today? To understand this shift, consider how the advent of the smartphone revolutionized communication. Similarly, the rise of personal automobiles profoundly changed how Americans view travel, casting aside the romance of the rails in favor of speed and individual freedom. While we no longer need to rely on timetables and shared journeys, the intricate network of roads and burgeoning car culture came with its own set of challenges—pollution, congestion, and the gradual erosion of communal experiences that trains once offered.

As we grapple with modern-day transportation challenges—congested highways, environmental concerns, and urban sprawl—the story of American passenger rail takes on renewed relevance. In this context, it's crucial to engage with provocative questions that invite reflection about the future. Can American passenger rail reclaim its place as a viable transportation option? What would it take for trains to become not just a nostalgic memory but a cornerstone of modern, sustainable transit systems?

Globally, other countries have embraced rail travel as a solution to many of the issues facing the United States today. High-speed trains zoom across Europe and Asia, linking cities in record time while minimizing environmental impact. These success stories offer lessons that could be invaluable in reshaping the future of American railroads. If nations like Japan and France can make high-speed rail work efficiently, why can't the United States? Exploring these international examples can provide fresh insights into what is possible and inspire a vision for an interconnected, sustainable future.

Join us as we take a journey through time— examining the splendor of the past, grappling with the challenges of today, and envisioning a sustainable, connected future. This book will not only illuminate the intricate tapestry of American rail history but also inspire reimagining its potential in a rapidly evolving transportation landscape. Each chapter delves into different facets of rail travel, from its historical roots to modern innovations and potential futures, offering a comprehensive look at where we've been and where we might go.

In the pages that follow, policy makers and urban planners will find data-driven discussions on how rail infrastructure improvements can serve as catalysts for broader societal benefits. Transportation enthusiasts will relish the detailed accounts of iconic trains and transformative moments in rail history. Academic scholars and students will discover a rich repository of information, bridging the gap between transportation studies, economics, and environmental science. By the end of this book, you will not only have a deeper appreciation for the rails but also a clearer vision of how they could redefine travel in America.

So whether you're a fan of the majestic locomotives that once crisscrossed our nation, a policy maker seeking sustainable solutions, or an academic delving into the nuances of public transport systems, there's something here for you. As we stand at the crossroads of innovation and tradition, one must ask: Can we breathe new life into American rail travel? What lessons can we glean from global success stories to reshape the future of our railroads?

Let's embark on this exploration together, merging the romance of the past with the practicality of modern needs, and perhaps, reignite a nation's love affair with trains. Welcome aboard.

Chapter Two

The Golden Age of American Passenger Rail

T he Golden Age of American passenger rail marked a period of remarkable growth and transformation in the transportation landscape of the United States. It was an era where the visionaries behind the railroads changed not only how people traveled but also how they perceived distances and connections within the country. This chapter delves into the early success and profound significance of American passenger railroads, highlighting the pivotal roles played by key figures whose innovative strategies and relentless determination helped shape this golden age.

In exploring this vibrant period, the chapter examines the contributions of influential individuals like Cornelius Vanderbilt and Leland Stanford, who were instrumental in building a robust rail network that spanned the nation. The narrative will unravel how their strategic approaches to railroad development created new opportunities for economic growth, regional connectivity, and social change. From the introduction of cutting-edge technologies and infrastructure improvements to the socio-economic impacts of increased mobility and cultural exchange, this section offers a comprehensive look at how American passenger railroads left an indelible mark on the nation's history and development.

Introduction to Early Rail Pioneers

The story of American passenger railroads is deeply entwined with the visionary endeavors of a few key figures whose innovative approaches and competitive spirit laid the foundation for what would become an enduring transportation legacy. Among these pioneers, Cornelius Vanderbilt and Leland Stanford stand out as emblematic figures whose contributions significantly shaped the early success and significance of American passenger railroads.

Cornelius Vanderbilt, often referred to as "The Commodore," was a business tycoon who recognized the immense potential of railroad travel during the mid-19th century. Initially making his fortune in shipping, Vanderbilt transitioned to railroads by investing in and eventually consolidating several key rail lines. His strategic vision enabled him to create an extensive network that connected major cities across the Eastern United States. One of his most notable achievements was the New York Central Railroad, which became a model of efficiency and profitability under his leadership.

Vanderbilt's innovative strategies were grounded in both financial acumen and operational foresight. To build his rail empire, he utilized horizontal integration, where he acquired competing rail lines and amalgamated them into a more cohesive and streamlined operation. This approach not only reduced competition but also allowed for standardized practices, improved schedules, and better maintenance of infrastructure. His focus on efficiency did not stop at consolidation; Vanderbilt was also instrumental in introducing new technologies and practices, such as steel rails and more powerful locomotives, which enhanced the safety and speed of rail travel.

On the other side of the continent, Leland Stanford played a critical role in the development of the Transcontinental Railroad, a project that symbolized the unity and expansion of the United States. As a central figure in the "Big Four" investors who financed and built the Central Pacific Railroad, Stanford's contributions were pivotal in connecting the eastern rail networks with the western United States. This monumental project required not only substantial capital but also significant political maneuvering, which Stanford adeptly managed through his roles as California Governor and U.S. Senator.

Stanford's approach differed from Vanderbilt's in many ways, particularly in his emphasis on community engagement and labor relations. While Vanderbilt focused on consolidation and efficiency, Stanford prioritized the human element of railroad construction. He employed thousands of workers, including a large number of Chinese immigrants, whose labor was crucial to overcoming the challenging terrain of the Sierra Nevada mountains. Despite facing numerous obstacles, including harsh weather conditions and difficult engineering challenges, Stanford's leadership ensured the timely completion of the Transcontinental Railroad, which transformed the American landscape by making coast-to-coast travel feasible.

The interaction between these influential figures was marked by a blend of competition and collaboration that spurred advancements in the railroad industry. Vanderbilt, with his control over the Eastern rail lines, and Stanford, with his influence on the Western front, both had vested interests in ensuring their respective networks thrived. However, they also recognized the mutual benefits of collaboration. For example, the Transcontinental Railroad was a joint effort between multiple rail companies that required synchronization and cooperation, illustrating that even fierce competitors could find common ground when faced with a shared objective.

Furthermore, the impact of Vanderbilt and Stanford extended beyond the confines of their rail empires, influencing the broader socio-economic environment of their era. The railroads they built facilitated unprecedented levels of mobility, enabling people to travel faster and farther than ever before. This newfound accessibility opened up economic opportunities, allowing goods to be transported efficiently across vast distances, thereby reducing costs and fostering trade. Cities and towns along the rail lines experienced rapid growth, becoming bustling hubs of commerce and industry. The railroads also played a key role in westward expansion, providing a vital link that encouraged settlement and development in previously remote areas.

In addition to economic prosperity, the railroads brought about significant social changes. They bridged geographic barriers, promoting cultural exchange and greater national cohesion. People from diverse backgrounds found themselves interconnected by a web of rail lines, facilitating the flow of ideas and cultures. Moreover, the railroads democratized travel, making it accessible to a broader segment of the population and transforming leisure and tourism in America.

The legacies of Cornelius Vanderbilt and Leland Stanford are evident not only in the physical infrastructure they helped build but also in the lasting impact they had on American society. Their vision and tenacity laid the groundwork for a transportation network that would revolutionize the way people moved, worked, and lived. As we reflect on the golden age of American passenger rail, it is essential to recognize the indelible marks left by these pioneering figures, whose efforts helped shape a nation on the move.

Impact of Transcontinental Railroads on Westward Expansion

The establishment of transcontinental railroads was a pivotal development in American history, profoundly influencing the westward migration and settlement. This monumental achievement, which connected the East Coast to the West Coast, accelerated the nation's growth and reshaped its social and economic landscape.

Manifest Destiny played a crucial role in driving the expansion of these railroads. Manifest Destiny was the belief that Americans were destined by God to expand their territory across the continent. The railroads became a tangible embodiment of this ideology. By providing an efficient mode of transportation, they made it feasible for people to move westward in search of new opportunities. Settlers were now able to traverse vast distances quickly and safely, reinforcing the notion that the United States was meant to stretch from coast to coast. The railroads symbolized progress and the realization of America's manifest destiny, providing a practical means to fulfill this ideological aspiration.

Economic opportunities flourished with the advent of the railroads. The expansive rail network opened up previously inaccessible areas, making it possible to exploit natural resources and develop new industries. Mining for gold and silver boomed as railroads provided a reliable way to transport valuable minerals to markets. Agriculture also saw significant growth; farmers could now ship their produce to distant markets, leading to increased production and profitability. Towns and cities sprang up along the railroad routes, becoming hubs of commerce and activity. These burgeoning settlements offered jobs and attracted businesses, stimulating local economies and contributing to national growth.

Transportation and accessibility underwent a dramatic transformation with the construction of the transcontinental railroads. Before the railroads, traveling from the East Coast to the West Coast was a grueling journey that could take months. With the completion of the first transcontinental railroad in

1869, the same trip could be made in just a week. This marked a revolutionary change in travel and logistics. Goods and people could move swiftly across the country, fostering trade and communication. The railroads facilitated the movement of troops and supplies during conflicts, proving to be a strategic asset. They also enabled the postal service to operate more efficiently, ensuring timely delivery of mail and packages. The enhanced connectivity brought the nation closer together, knitting diverse regions into a cohesive whole.

Cultural exchange was another significant impact of the railroads. As people moved westward, they brought with them their customs, traditions, and ways of life. This mingling of cultures led to a rich tapestry of diversity in the American West. Immigrants from Europe, Asia, and other parts of the world played a crucial role in constructing the railroads, and their influence can still be seen in the cultural fabric of the region. Festivals, cuisines, languages, and religious practices from different parts of the world enriched the cultural landscape. The railroads acted as conduits for ideas and innovations, spreading knowledge and fostering understanding among various communities. This cultural blending helped shape a unique American identity, characterized by its multiculturalism and openness to new influences.

Peter Wretzky

Technological Innovations in the Railway Sector

The Golden Age of American passenger rail was marked by significant technological advancements that revolutionized the industry and enhanced its efficiency. One of the most notable areas of progress was in locomotive development. During this period, steam locomotives underwent substantial evolution, leading to engines that were more powerful, faster, and capable of covering longer distances without frequent stops. Early steam engines were relatively simple machines, but by the mid-19th century, engineers had introduced advancements such as improved boiler designs, efficient fuel combustion systems, and better traction control. These enhancements allowed trains to pull heavier loads while maintaining higher speeds, making rail travel more reliable and appealing to both passengers and freight customers.

Another major advancement came with the development of diesel-electric locomotives in the 20th century. Diesel engines offered numerous advantages over their steam counterparts. They were more fuel-efficient, required less maintenance, and could be operated more easily by a smaller crew. The introduction of diesel-electric technology marked a shift in the industry, further improving operational efficiency and reducing costs.

Signal systems also saw remarkable advancements during the golden age of American passenger rail. Early railroads relied on basic, manually-operated signaling methods, which often led to accidents and delays. The introduction of electric signals represented a quantum leap in safety and efficiency. Electric signal systems made it possible to control train movements more precisely and communicate effectively between stations. Advances like block signaling, where the track was divided into segments or "blocks" each controlled by signals, helped prevent collisions by ensuring that only one train occupied a given section of track at any time. This method greatly reduced the risk of accidents and allowed trains to operate closer together, increasing the overall capacity of the network.

Further enhancements in signaling included interlocking systems, which coordinated signals and switches to ensure safe and optimal routing of trains through complex track layouts. These systems replaced manual switch-tenders and flagmen, providing an automated and reliable way to manage rail traffic. The advent of centralized traffic control (CTC), which allowed a single operator to oversee large sections of track from a central location, brought about even greater improvements. CTC not only enhanced safety but also improved scheduling and efficiency, enabling railroads to offer more reliable service.

Peter Wretzky

The evolution of track and infrastructure played a critical role in the success of American passenger railroads. In the early days, tracks were constructed from wrought iron, which was prone to wear and tear. However, the adoption of steel rails in the latter half of the 19th century marked a significant improvement. Steel is far more durable and capable of supporting heavier loads, thus increasing the lifespan and reliability of railroad tracks. Additionally, the development of the Bessemer process for mass-producing steel made it more affordable, facilitating widespread upgrades across the rail network.

Infrastructure projects such as bridges, tunnels, and viaducts also saw considerable advancements. Engineers designed and built structures that could support the weight and speed of modern trains, connecting regions that had previously been difficult to access. For example, the construction of the transcontinental railroad, which linked the eastern and western United States, involved the creation of numerous engineering marvels, including the famous Horseshoe Curve in Pennsylvania and the intricate series of tunnels and snow sheds that traversed the Sierra Nevada mountains. These infrastructural developments not only improved the efficiency of rail travel but also opened up new economic opportunities by connecting distant markets.

Safety innovations were another crucial aspect of the golden age of American passenger rail. The increasing speed and frequency of train services necessitated new approaches to ensuring passenger and worker safety. One of the most significant safety advancements was the introduction of the Westinghouse air brake system. Unlike the older handbrake method, which required train crews to manually apply brakes on each car, the air brake system used compressed air to activate brakes simultaneously across the entire train. This invention drastically reduced stopping distances and allowed for safer, more controlled deceleration, especially on long and heavy trains.

Other safety innovations included the development of automatic couplers, which replaced the dangerous practice of manually connecting train cars with link-and-pin couplings. Automatic couplers not only reduced the risk of injury but also sped up the process of assembling and disassembling trains, thereby improving operational efficiency. Additionally, the implementation of standardized time zones helped coordinate train schedules more effectively, reducing instances of collision caused by miscommunication or timing errors.

Peter Wretzky

Cultural Significance of Rail Travel in America

American passenger railroads didn't just transform transportation; they reshaped American culture, identity, and leisure. They symbolized progress, creating new ways for people to connect socially while boosting the tourism industry.

The railroads quickly became a symbol of progress. As iron rails stretched across vast distances, they embodied the spirit of American innovation and growth. Trains were faster than anything that had come before, significantly cutting travel time across the nation. This technological leap forward resonated deeply with the American public, signifying a country on the move. The advent of the railroad was often depicted in literature, art, and media, capturing the imagination of a people eager to embrace the future. Railroads represented not just physical progress but also economic and industrial advancements, contributing to America's burgeoning identity as an innovative powerhouse.

The social connections facilitated by rail travel brought Americans closer together in ways not previously imagined. Before railroads, many communities remained isolated due to poor road conditions and limited modes of transport. Railroads bridged these gaps, making distant regions feel like close neighbors. Families could visit each other more frequently, and business relationships could thrive over longer distances. Moreover, train stations themselves became social hubs. People gathered there not just to travel, but to meet, converse, and engage in community activities. This increased mobility played a significant role in fostering a sense of national unity, helping to build a shared cultural identity.

Next, the impact of railroads on tourism cannot be overlooked. As rail networks expanded, so did opportunities for leisure travel. People who once considered long-distance travel impractical now found it accessible and affordable. This was a groundbreaking shift, enabling Americans to explore their own country in unprecedented ways. Tourist destinations sprang up along railway lines, supported by promotional campaigns by railroad companies. These companies often offered package deals that included lodging and guided tours, encouraging travel to scenic and historic locations. The Grand Tour of Europe was soon rivaled by America's own itineraries, such as journeys through the Rockies or visits to National Parks. The rise of leisure travel fed back into the economy, promoting the hospitality industry and local craftspeople.

With this surge in tourism came iconic rail journeys that captured the nation's imagination. Certain routes became legendary, celebrated for their breathtaking scenery or the unique experiences they offered. For example, the California Zephyr's route from Chicago to San Francisco traverses spectacular landscapes, including the Rocky Mountains and the Sierra Nevada. These trips weren't just about reaching a destination; they were immersive experiences that showcased the diverse beauty of the nation. In the East, the Crescent Route offered another famous journey, traveling from New York City through the Southern states down to New Orleans. Such routes provided not only transportation but a window into different lifestyles, cultures, and geographies, enriching the travelers' understanding of their country.

Thus, the railroads influenced American life far beyond mere transportation. They became a symbol of what the country could achieve through ingenuity and hard work. They connected people, fostered social interaction, and shaped a shared cultural experience. By opening up new horizons for tourism, they helped Americans discover their own homeland in ways that were both profound and leisurely enjoyable. Iconic rail journeys allowed passengers to experience the country's natural beauty and cultural diversity firsthand, creating memories and stories that have been passed down through generations.

Economic Contributions During the Late 19th and Early 20th Centuries

The economic impact of passenger railroads on the American economy during their peak years was profound and multifaceted. One of the most significant contributions was job creation. Railroads were a major source of employment, helping to build and sustain the burgeoning American workforce. From the construction of the tracks to the operation of the trains, vast numbers of workers found steady employment. This included engineers, conductors, ticket agents, maintenance crews, and many other roles essential to the functioning of a robust rail network.

The ripple effect of job creation extended beyond direct employment. Ancillary businesses and services sprang up in support of the railroads. This included everything from manufacturing companies producing railcars and locomotives to hospitality services catering to travelers. The demand for labor was not confined to one sector; it permeated various industries, fostering a diverse range of job opportunities across the nation.

Turning to the impact on industries, the railroads played a crucial role in bolstering several key sectors of the American economy. For instance, the steel industry saw substantial growth due to the enormous demand for rails, locomotives, and bridges. Ironworks expanded rapidly as they sought to meet the needs of the railway companies, leading to innovations in smelting and metal production techniques. Similarly, the coal industry thrived since steam locomotives depended heavily on coal as fuel. Mines proliferated, and there was an increased need for miners and related professionals.

Agriculture benefited significantly from the advent of railroads. Farmers could transport their goods to markets far faster and more efficiently than ever before, reducing spoilage and increasing profitability. Grain, livestock, and perishable goods such as fruits and vegetables could now reach urban centers quickly, where burgeoning populations eagerly consumed them. This ability to move produce over long distances at relatively low cost opened new markets and encouraged farmers to increase production, knowing that transportation bottlenecks were being alleviated by the expanding rail network.

Railroads also catalyzed regional development, transforming local economies and spurring urbanization. Towns and cities sprouted along rail lines, turning previously isolated areas into bustling hubs of commerce and trade. Regions with direct rail access experienced economic booms as businesses flocked to these new population centers. Real estate values soared around rail stations, and investments poured into infrastructure projects to support the growing communities. Urban planners of the time recognized the strategic importance of rail connectivity, which often dictated the planning and expansion of metropolitan areas.

A notable example of this phenomenon is the city of Chicago. Its strategic location as a rail hub connecting the East and West coasts transformed it into a critical commercial center. Within a few short decades, Chicago evolved from a small town into one of the largest and most economically vibrant cities in the United States. The railroad's influence on regional development cannot be overstated; it redefined geographic and economic landscapes across the country.

International trade dynamics were similarly revolutionized by the introduction and expansion of railroads. Before the advent of comprehensive rail networks, moving goods from inland production areas to port cities was time-consuming and costly. Railroads bridged this gap, enabling swift and efficient transportation of exports to coastal ports where they could be shipped overseas. This development facilitated a dramatic increase in the volume and speed of trade, solidifying America's position in the global market.

Exports of raw materials like cotton, timber, and minerals surged as railroads provided reliable means of transporting these commodities to international buyers. Additionally, imports of foreign goods became more accessible to interior regions of the country, no longer restricted by the limitations of river or canal transport. The flow of global goods into and out of American markets laid the groundwork for the country's burgeoning industrial economy, which would eventually establish the United States as a dominant player on the world stage.

Furthermore, the synergies between railroads and other emerging technologies accelerated economic growth. Telegraph lines often paralleled railroad tracks, bringing communication advancements that synced with the physical movement of goods and people. The combination of instantaneous communication and rapid transport was a powerful catalyst for both domestic and international business operations. Transactions could be negotiated and goods dispatched with unprecedented efficiency, marking a new era in economic activity.

Summary and Reflections

The early success and significance of American passenger railroads were largely influenced by the visionary efforts of key figures like Cornelius Vanderbilt and Leland Stanford. Their contributions helped shape a robust transportation network that connected the nation, fostering economic growth and societal changes. Vanderbilt's strategic consolidations and innovative practices in the East, combined with Stanford's monumental work on the Transcontinental Railroad in the West, collectively laid the foundation for an efficient and expansive rail system. These developments enabled unprecedented levels of mobility, facilitating trade, travel, and cultural exchanges across vast distances.

Through their endeavors, these pioneers not only revolutionized transportation but also spurred dramatic economic and social transformations. Railroads made it possible to transport goods swiftly and affordably, opening new markets and boosting local economies. This increased accessibility encouraged urban development and the settlement of remote areas, effectively shaping America's landscape. Moreover, the railroads bridged geographic barriers, promoting national cohesion and cultural understanding. The legacy of American passenger railroads, marked by innovation and tenacity, continues to influence modern transportation systems, highlighting the enduring impact of these early advancements on contemporary society.

Chapter Three

The Downfall Begins: Post-War Decline

T he shift towards automobiles in post-war America marked the beginning of a significant transformation in the nation's transportation landscape. This chapter delves into the myriad factors that contributed to the decline of American passenger railroads during the mid-20th century, setting the stage for understanding the current state of rail travel. As Americans returned from World War II, cultural preferences began to shift, and the autonomy and convenience provided by personal vehicles quickly gained widespread appeal. This change was propelled by suburban expansion, making car ownership indispensable for daily life, fundamentally altering travel patterns and reducing reliance on trains.

In addition to the rise of automobile culture, this chapter also examines the role of government policies and infrastructure developments that favored road transport over railways. The establishment of the Interstate Highway System further entrenched the dominance of cars, drawing both passengers and freight away from railroads. Competition from the burgeoning airline industry offered another fast and efficient mode of travel, further diminishing the attractiveness of rail services. Economic challenges and declining investments in rail infrastructure compounded these issues, creating a vicious cycle of reduced ridership and service quality. The chapter provides a comprehensive overview of these intersecting elements, offering insights into the historical context that has shaped contemporary discussions about rail transport.

Rise of Automobile Culture

The cultural shift towards automobiles in post-war America significantly contributed to the decline of passenger rail services. This period saw a dramatic change in consumer behavior, which had profound impacts on rail ridership.

One of the primary factors driving this shift was the post-war suburban expansion. As suburbs grew, car ownership became increasingly essential for daily commuting and running errands. The convenience of owning a personal vehicle eliminated the dependency on train schedules, making cars the preferred mode of transportation. Suburban neighborhoods were often designed without easy access to public transit, further encouraging residents to rely on their automobiles. The widespread availability of affordable housing outside city centers attracted many families, reinforcing the trend towards car ownership as people moved further from urban cores.

Automobiles quickly became a symbol of personal freedom and were marketed as an integral part of the American Dream. Car manufacturers capitalized on this sentiment through aggressive advertising campaigns that depicted cars as gateways to independence and adventure. Owning a car was portrayed as not just practical but aspirational, representing success and modernity. This powerful imagery sidelined public transit options like trains, which did not evoke the same sense of liberty or status. Advertisements frequently highlighted the ability to travel on one's own schedule, explore new places effortlessly, and avoid the crowded, less glamorous conditions associated with train travel.

In addition to cultural shifts, technological and economic developments made cars more accessible to the average American. The mass production methods refined during World War II were repurposed to manufacture automobiles, leading to a significant reduction in costs. As cars became more affordable, they were no longer a luxury item reserved for the wealthy. Middle-class families could now purchase vehicles, fundamentally altering public perceptions of travel convenience. Trains, bound by fixed tracks and schedules, seemed less flexible compared to the door-to-door service provided by cars. This newfound accessibility meant that families could travel at their own pace, stop whenever they wanted, and carry more luggage—all advantages that made cars increasingly desirable over trains.

The demographics of rail users also shifted during this time. Younger generations, who had grown up during or after the war, embraced driving over using public transport. For these individuals, cars were more than just a means of getting around; they represented a rite of passage and a step towards adulthood. Teenagers and young adults viewed driving as a crucial skill and an essential part of their social life. The allure of road trips, drive-in theaters, and the culture surrounding cars resonated more with them than the structured environment of rail travel. As a result, traditional rail ridership declined, with fewer younger passengers opting for trains.

The combined impact of these factors created a feedback loop that further entrenched the preference for automobiles. The rising popularity of cars led to increased investments in road infrastructure, which in turn made driving even more convenient. Conversely, the declining number of train passengers resulted in reduced revenues for rail companies, limiting their ability to maintain and improve services. This decrease in quality made train travel less attractive, pushing even more people towards cars. Furthermore, the social aspect of driving—aided by media portrayals of road culture—cemented the automobile's place in American society. Movies, music, and literature from the era romanticized the open road and the freedom it offered, embedding these ideas deeply into the national consciousness.

For example, the growth of roadside attractions and motels catered to travelers, creating an ecosystem that supported and encouraged automotive travel. These establishments were often located near major highways and became destinations themselves, offering convenience and entertainment that further diminished the appeal of trains. Families planning vacations opted for road trips, enjoying the flexibility cars provided to explore various sights without the constraints of train routes and timetables.

Also noteworthy is how the economic landscape influenced consumer choices. Post-war prosperity brought about higher disposable incomes, enabling more families to afford cars. This economic boom was accompanied by a surge in consumerism, with people eager to spend on goods that enhanced their lifestyle. Cars, often seen as a status symbol, fit perfectly into this narrative. The ability to customize and choose specific models added to the car's allure, something that trains could not offer. As car culture flourished, it became a key aspect of American identity, marginalizing alternatives like rail travel.

Consumer behavior changes were also evident in the way people planned their daily commutes and leisure activities. The preference for cars over trains was visible in the design of cities and towns, which increasingly prioritized road networks over rail lines. Urban planning decisions favored parking spaces, wide roads, and highways, making driving more convenient. Public transit options were often neglected, creating a cycle where decreased usage led to underinvestment and further decline in service quality.

Moreover, the rise of shopping centers and malls, typically situated outside city centers, facilitated by ample parking, underscored the dominance of car culture. These new commercial hubs drew shoppers away from downtown areas traditionally served by trains, contributing to the reduced necessity for rail travel. The ability to load purchases directly into a car reinforced the practicality and convenience of driving versus taking the train.

Expansion of the Interstate Highway System

The creation of the Interstate Highway System in the mid-20th century marked a pivotal transition in the transportation landscape of America, significantly influencing the decline of passenger railroads. This development reshaped not only the nation's infrastructure but also its travel priorities, as government policies began to heavily favor road transport over railways. One of the most significant impacts of this shift was the reallocation of federal investment. Resources that could have been used to modernize and maintain rail infrastructure were instead funneled into building an extensive network of highways. This redirection of funds fundamentally redefined the country's transportation priorities, reinforcing a preference for personal and freight mobility via roads.

The appeal of interstate highways was immediate and profound. The smoothness and speed of highway travel presented an attractive alternative to the slower, often less direct train journeys. Highways facilitated quicker commutes between cities and within regions, appealing to a populace increasingly enamored with the idea of rapid, flexible travel. For many Americans, the convenience of hopping into a car and driving directly to their destination without the limitations imposed by train schedules and routes became highly desirable. This allure significantly contributed to declining rail passenger numbers as more people opted for the freedom and efficiency offered by highway travel.

Another critical outcome of the Interstate Highway System was its role in promoting suburban growth. Before the highways, many Americans lived in densely populated urban areas where public transit, including trains, was convenient and necessary. However, the new highways made living outside crowded city centers both feasible and attractive. Suburbs began to flourish, pulling people away from urban cores and train stations. With fewer people relying on trains for their daily commute, the demand for passenger rail services dwindled. Large swathes of the population no longer found it necessary to live near rail lines, leading to a decentralization of population density that further eroded the relevance of passenger railroads.

The expansion of the highway system did not only affect passenger traffic; it also had dire consequences for freight transport via rail. Railroads, which had traditionally carried a substantial portion of the nation's goods, started losing freight revenue to the burgeoning trucking industry. Trucks offered versatile and often faster delivery options directly to various destinations without the need to transfer goods between different modes of transport. This shift placed additional financial strain on rail companies, many of which had already begun seeing a decrease in passenger revenue. As trucks took over a larger share of freight transport, railroads faced diminishing returns, making it even harder to invest in and maintain rail infrastructure.

Governmental decisions played a crucial role in fostering this transportation evolution. The Federal-Aid Highway Act of 1956 allocated unprecedented amounts of money to construct and expand the highway network. Lawmakers believed that a robust interstate system was essential for national defense and economic growth, thereby justifying the immense expenditure. However, this focus came at the expense of the railroads, which received comparatively little support for modernization or expansion. Without adequate funding, railroads struggled to compete with the modern, well-funded highway infrastructure. This lack of investment led to deteriorating rail conditions, which only reinforced the public's perception that trains were an outdated mode of transportation.

The adverse effects on railroads were cumulative and self-perpetuating. As rail services declined in quality due to insufficient funding and maintenance, fewer people chose to travel by train, leading to further losses in revenue. This cycle of decline made it increasingly difficult for railroads to justify or afford the necessary upgrades to attract passengers back. While highways continued to receive ample funding and development, railroads languished, unable to keep up with the evolving transportation needs of the nation.

Suburban growth spurred by highways also had broader implications for urban planning and development. Communities spread out over larger areas, requiring extensive road networks to connect homes, businesses, and amenities. This layout made it challenging to integrate efficient public transit systems, including rail, into the growing suburban sprawl. Planners focused more on accommodating car travel than on preserving or enhancing rail accessibility. As a result, the physical infrastructure developed around automobiles, further isolating rail users and diminishing the practicality of maintaining extensive passenger rail services.

Even as railroads attempted to innovate and compete, they faced insurmountable challenges. Efforts to streamline operations, reduce travel times, and improve service quality were often undermined by the entrenched advantages of highway travel. The disparity in governmental support meant that railroads were always playing catch-up, struggling with outdated technology and insufficient funding. This imbalance highlighted a broader issue of policy direction, where long-term sustainability and diversity in transportation options were sacrificed for short-term economic gains and the perceived benefits of automobile-centric development.

Peter Wretzky

Competition from the Airline Industry

The latter half of the 20th century marked a seismic shift in America's transportation landscape, driven in large part by the rise of air travel. This transformation dramatically impacted passenger rail services, once the backbone of intercity travel. The advent of affordable air travel played a significant role in this dynamic change.

With the introduction of jet aircraft in the late 1950s and early 1960s, airlines began to offer faster, more efficient means of travel over long distances at increasingly competitive prices. Prior to this, railroads had dominated intercity travel, providing a reliable and relatively comfortable mode of transit. However, the speed of planes, which could cover distances in hours that trains took days to traverse, suddenly made air travel an enticing option for many Americans. As ticket prices decreased due to economies of scale and technological advancements, flying became accessible to a broader segment of the population. This democratization of air travel expanded the reach of airlines, allowing them to infiltrate markets previously monopolized by rail services.

Targeting these profitable rail corridors was a strategic move for airlines seeking to maximize their revenue streams. Major routes such as New York to

Chicago or Los Angeles to San Francisco, historically strongholds of passenger rail, saw intensive competition from airlines. These high-demand routes were essential lifelines for rail companies, contributing significantly to their profitability. By capturing a substantial share of passengers on these routes, airlines not only increased their market presence but also destabilized the financial foundations of railroad companies. The loss of passengers on these lucrative routes forced railroads to slash services or altogether abandon certain lines, which only further accelerated their decline.

The competitive edge of airlines extended beyond merely providing an alternative mode of transportation. Airlines invested heavily in marketing campaigns that reshaped public perception of travel. Through aggressive advertising, they painted air travel as the epitome of modernity and luxury. Flying was not just about getting from point A to point B; it was marketed as an experience—an adventure in itself. Sleek advertisements showcased glamorous stewardesses, spacious cabins, and the allure of soaring above the clouds, cultivating an image of sophistication and convenience. This branding starkly contrasted with the often outdated and cumbersome nature of train travel, making trains appear less appealing, especially to younger, more affluent travelers eager to embrace modern trends.

Additionally, investments in airport infrastructure played a crucial role in enhancing the appeal of air travel. Federal and local governments poured resources into building and expanding airports, equipping them with state-of-the-art facilities designed to streamline the passenger experience. Modern terminals featured amenities like expansive waiting areas, duty-free shops, and efficient luggage handling systems, creating a seamless and attractive travel environment. In contrast, many train stations struggled with aging infrastructure that failed to keep pace with passenger expectations. The disparity between gleaming new airports and dilapidated rail stations further tilted the balance in favor of air travel. Passengers naturally gravitated towards the fresher, more efficient options offered by airlines.

The cumulative effect of these factors was a profound shift in the nation's transportation preferences. The multi-pronged strategy adopted by airlines—the affordability of air travel, targeting key rail corridors, innovative marketing, and investment in superior infrastructure—collectively undermined the dominance of railroads. For American passenger rail, this period marked the beginning of a relegation to a secondary role in the national travel narrative.

As air travel soared, many rail companies found themselves in a financial quagmire. They were compelled to make difficult decisions, including cutting back on less profitable routes, reducing services, and deferring maintenance and upgrades. This vicious cycle only worsened the quality and reliability of rail services, driving even more passengers towards the burgeoning airline industry.

Moreover, the broader implications of this transformation extended beyond the economic struggles of rail companies. The shift away from rail travel altered the socio-economic framework of communities built around rail hubs. Towns and cities that had thrived due to their connectivity via rail faced economic downturns as passenger numbers dwindled. The rail industry's decline had a cascading effect, influencing urban planning, real estate markets, and even local employment patterns tied to rail operations.

In examining this transformative period, it's clear that the ascendancy of air travel redefined how Americans perceived and utilized their transportation options. The intricate dance between emerging airlines and established railroads set the stage for a radically different transportation environment, the repercussions of which are still felt in contemporary discussions about sustainable transport solutions and infrastructural development.

Peter Wretzky

Declining Investments in Rail Infrastructure

In the aftermath of World War II, American passenger railroads faced numerous obstacles that collectively led to their decline. One prominent issue was the aging infrastructure that suffered from years of inadequate maintenance and minimal upgrading efforts. Many tracks, trains, and station facilities were relics of an earlier era, struggling to keep up with contemporary demands for speed, comfort, and reliability. Tracks often became warped or misaligned, leading to frequent delays and safety concerns. Trains themselves were antiquated, lacking modern conveniences that were becoming commonplace in other modes of transportation. The overall experience for passengers deteriorated significantly, making train travel less attractive to a population seeking efficiency and convenience.

The situation worsened as government funding increasingly favored road infrastructure over public transportation investments. In a landscape dominated by the burgeoning popularity of the automobile, policymakers redirected financial resources toward the construction and expansion of highways. This shift reflected a broader national agenda that prioritized car travel and suburban development. The Federal-Aid Highway Act of 1956 epitomized this trend, channeling billions of dollars into creating an extensive interstate highway system. While this was a boon for motorists, it came at the expense of railroads, which saw their share of government support diminish considerably. This reallocation of funds signaled a stark change in priorities, with rail infrastructure improvements falling by the wayside.

Private sector disengagement also played a critical role in the decline of American passenger railroads. Historically, private rail companies had been instrumental in developing and maintaining extensive rail networks across the country. However, as profits dwindled and operating costs soared, these companies began to withdraw their financial commitment to rail infrastructure. Investments in modernization and improvement projects became rare, further exacerbating the problems already posed by aging infrastructure. The competitive pressures from automobiles and airlines made it increasingly difficult for private rail companies to justify substantial investments in a mode of transport that was losing its market share. Consequently, the stagnation of rail technology and services continued unabated.

As financial support waned, both government and private sector investment in rail infrastructure dwindled. This lack of funding led to a noticeable decline in service levels and routes available to passengers. Railroads found it challenging to maintain existing lines, let alone expand or enhance them. Timetables became less reliable, with fewer trains running on schedule. Routes that were once popular and heavily trafficked started to see reduced frequency or were abandoned altogether. This reduction in service prompted many potential travelers to seek alternative forms of transportation, perpetuating a cycle of declining ridership and service degradation. With fewer passengers using the trains, revenue dropped even further, creating a vicious cycle where diminishing financial resources led to poorer service, which in turn drove away more customers.

Union Strikes and Labor Issues

Labor strikes and ongoing labor disputes were significant factors that affected the operations of American passenger railroads in the mid-20th century. These issues often caused major disruptions in service, frustrating passengers and diminishing their trust in the reliability of rail travel. Frequent labor disputes typically led to sudden halts in rail services, stranding passengers and causing widespread inconvenience. The unpredictability of train schedules due to these strikes made it challenging for travelers to rely on trains for timely transportation, prompting many to seek alternative modes of travel.

The push for better wages and job security among rail workers created operational inefficiencies and financial constraints for rail companies. Rail employees, including conductors, engineers, and maintenance crews, demanded fair compensation for their labor, which they argued was crucial given the demanding nature of their work. However, meeting these demands often resulted in higher operating costs for rail companies, who struggled to balance payroll expenses with declining revenues. Negotiations over wages and benefits frequently stalled, leading to prolonged disputes that further hampered the smooth functioning of rail services.

These operational inefficiencies became more pronounced as rail companies attempted to modernize amidst evolving labor demographics. The post-war era saw significant changes in the workforce, with an increasing number of younger, more diverse laborers entering the industry. This shift necessitated adjustments in labor practices, including updated training programs and revised safety protocols. Yet, the financial burdens imposed by ongoing labor disputes made it difficult for rail companies to implement these necessary changes effectively. As a result, many railroads found themselves stuck in a cycle of outdated practices and inadequate working conditions, further exacerbating their decline.

Moreover, labor issues significantly contributed to the negative public image of railroads during this period. Media coverage of strikes and disputes often painted rail companies as unreliable and inefficient, reinforcing public perceptions of trains as an impractical option for transportation. Stories of stranded passengers and canceled journeys became common, damaging the reputation of railroads and deterring potential riders. As the public's trust in rail services eroded, so did ridership numbers, creating a feedback loop of declining revenue and service quality.

The friction between labor demands and management capabilities also led to internal instability within rail companies. Management teams were caught between the need to maintain profitability and the pressure to address the legitimate concerns of their workforce. This tension often manifested in inconsistent policies and fragmented efforts to improve working conditions, leaving employees dissatisfied and further destabilizing the industry. The lack of cohesive strategies to handle labor disputes effectively undermined efforts to modernize and adapt to changing market dynamics.

Financial constraints imposed by labor disputes not only affected day-to-day operations but also hindered long-term planning and investment in infrastructure improvements. With limited funds available, rail companies struggled to maintain existing tracks and facilities, let alone invest in new technologies or expand their networks. This stagnation meant that rail systems lagged behind other forms of transportation that were rapidly evolving, such as automobiles and later airlines. The inability to modernize compounded the challenges faced by railroads, making them less competitive in an increasingly diverse transportation market.

Additionally, the demographic shifts in the labor force brought about new expectations and attitudes toward work-life balance and job satisfaction. Younger generations entering the rail industry were often less willing to endure the grueling hours and harsh conditions that had characterized earlier periods. This change necessitated a reevaluation of labor practices, yet the financial strain from ongoing disputes made it difficult to enact meaningful reforms. Consequently, rail companies found themselves grappling with high turnover rates and a disengaged workforce, which further impacted operational efficiency and service reliability.

Public perception of railroads as unreliable was not merely a consequence of media portrayal; it was also rooted in the lived experiences of passengers who faced frequent delays and cancellations. The cumulative effect of these negative experiences fostered a sense of disillusionment with rail travel, prompting many to consider alternative modes of transportation that seemed less prone to disruption. The rise of personal vehicles and later the expansion of air travel offered compelling alternatives for those seeking reliable and convenient transportation options, accelerating the decline in rail ridership.

Economic pressures stemming from labor disputes also forced rail companies to make difficult choices regarding resource allocation. In many cases, funds that might have been directed toward improving infrastructure or expanding services were instead diverted to cover increased labor costs or settle disputes. This reallocation of resources stymied innovation and left little room for strategic investments that could have revitalized the industry. The cumulative impact of these financial decisions contributed to a downward spiral of declining service quality and diminished public confidence in rail travel.

The interplay between labor disputes and declining revenues created a vicious cycle that proved difficult for rail companies to break. As workforce tensions escalated, operational inefficiencies mounted, leading to further reductions in service quality and reliability. Passengers, frustrated by the constant disruptions, increasingly turned to other modes of transportation, resulting in lower ridership and decreased revenue streams. This, in turn, made it even more challenging for rail companies to address labor grievances effectively, perpetuating the cycle of decline.

Summary and Reflections

This chapter has explored the complex interplay of factors that contributed to the decline of American passenger railroads in the mid-20th century. The rise of automobile culture, suburban expansion, and strategic marketing by car manufacturers played significant roles in shifting public preference towards personal vehicles. Additionally, the development of the Interstate Highway System and substantial government investments in road infrastructure further marginalized rail travel. These changes reshaped urban planning and reinforced car dependency, making it challenging for railroads to compete.

Moreover, the growth of the airline industry introduced a new competitive landscape, drawing passengers away from trains with the promise of faster, more efficient travel. Declining investments in rail infrastructure, along with frequent labor disputes, exacerbated the situation, leading to service reductions and deteriorating conditions. Together, these elements created a feedback loop that solidified the dominance of cars and planes while relegating passenger rail to a secondary role. This historical context sets the stage for understanding current discussions about reviving and modernizing rail travel in America.

Chapter Four

Trying to Stay Afloat: The 1960s and 70s

P assenger rail services in the United States faced turbulent times during the 1960s and 70s, grappling with numerous challenges that threatened their very existence. As government policies began to favor the development of highways and air travel, railroads were left struggling with diminished financial support and dwindling ridership. These decades saw significant shifts in transportation preferences and policies that greatly influenced the fate of passenger rail services. The Federal Aid Highway Act of 1956 signaled a monumental shift in federal priorities, directing substantial funds towards highway construction and leaving railroads to fend for themselves. This lack of financial backing rendered many private rail companies unable to sustain their operations, leading to route closures and service reductions.

Within this context, states took varied approaches to attempt to preserve their regional rail services. Some states, recognizing the importance of these services for daily commuters, established organizations like New York's Metropolitan Transportation Authority (MTA) to subsidize and maintain rail lines. Meanwhile, the federal government's creation of Amtrak in 1971 was an essential step in salvaging national rail services. However, the establishment of Amtrak came with its own set of challenges, including inadequate funding and inherited infrastructure issues. Throughout the chapter, we will explore the impacts of government policy shifts, state-level interventions, the formation of Amtrak, and the broader social and economic implications of rail service cutbacks. We will also delve into the public perception of rail travel during this era, examining how accidents, competition, and marketing played roles in shaping opinions. Finally, the chapter will reflect on the notable failures and limited successes in attempts to revitalize passenger rail, providing valuable lessons for future transportation initiatives.

Government Policy Shifts

In the 1960s and 70s, government policies shifted significantly, affecting the fate of passenger rail services. Federal regulations during this period increasingly prioritized the development of highways and airlines over rail services. The Federal Aid Highway Act of 1956 marked a pivotal moment, diverting substantial funds to highway construction. This decision reflected a national enthusiasm for automobile travel and air travel but left passenger rail services grappling with diminished financial support.

As federal focus shifted, states took various approaches to sustain their regional rail services. States like New York and California recognized the importance of commuter and regional trains and attempted to subsidize these services to ensure their survival. For example, New York's Metropolitan Transportation Authority (MTA) was established in 1965 to save the declining commuter rail lines around New York City, which were vital for daily commuters. Despite these efforts, success varied widely across different regions. Some state interventions managed to provide modest relief and maintain essential services, while others struggled due to lack of resources or sufficient political will. For instance, while Massachusetts invested in Boston's public transit system, many rural areas saw reductions in service due to inadequate funding and dwindling ridership.

Amidst these challenges, the federal government's introduction of Amtrak legislation in 1970 marked a significant shift. The National Railroad Passenger Corporation, commonly known as Amtrak, was created to revitalize and manage the nation's intercity passenger rail service. Before Amtrak, private rail companies had been hemorrhaging money due to declining passenger numbers and increasing competition from cars and planes. The creation of Amtrak represented a recognition at the federal level that passenger rail still held value and could benefit from coordinated management and funding. Early on, Amtrak faced its own set of hurdles, including inherited dilapidated infrastructure and skepticism from both the public and policymakers. Nevertheless, it was a crucial step in preventing the complete collapse of passenger rail services.

Policies from this era didn't just address immediate needs; they also laid the groundwork for future transportation debates. The prioritization of highways and airports over railways has remained a point of contention among transportation experts, urban planners, and policymakers. Understanding the decisions made during the 1960s and 70s helps contextualize contemporary discussions about sustainable transportation solutions. These historical policies highlighted the need for balanced investment across different modes of transport, acknowledging that each has its unique benefits and challenges. Today's debates often circle back to the same questions: How much should we invest in maintaining and expanding rail services? What is the role of government versus private sector in providing these services? The groundwork laid by the policies of the 1960s and 70s continues to influence these ongoing discussions.

The era also saw emerging environmental awareness, which began influencing transportation policy. The Environmental Protection Agency (EPA) was established in 1970, reflecting growing concern about pollution and sustainability. Rail travel, being generally more energy-efficient and less polluting than car or air travel, started to be seen in a new light. Advocates began pushing for better funding and support for trains as a means to combat rising emissions. Despite limited immediate success, these advocacy efforts planted seeds for later developments in green transportation initiatives.

Moreover, the social and economic implications of diminished rail funding became apparent. Rail networks historically had provided critical connections between cities and rural areas, fostering economic growth and social mobility. Their decline led to isolation of some communities, increased traffic congestion in metropolitan areas, and greater reliance on fossil fuels. In this context, policy shifts of the 1960s and 70s not only influenced transportation patterns but also had broader socioeconomic and environmental impacts.

The intertwining issues of federal funding priorities, state-level interventions, the establishment of Amtrak, and the long-term policy legacies offer a multifaceted view of how government actions shaped the passenger rail industry. These factors underscore the complexity of sustaining such an infrastructure amidst changing political, economic, and social landscapes. They illustrate the delicate balance required in maintaining an equitable and efficient transportation system.

Formation of Amtrak

In an era marked by the rise of automobiles and the expansion of air travel, the American passenger rail industry faced a significant decline during the 1960s and 70s. The formation of Amtrak in 1971 emerged as a pivotal response to this downturn, aimed at salvaging national rail services and bolstering connectivity across the country. At its core, Amtrak was created to manage national rail routes with the goal of revitalizing what many saw as a dying mode of transportation.

Amtrak's inception was driven by the need to maintain essential rail services that private companies could no longer sustain. The government envisioned a centralized body that could streamline operations and ensure continuity. Initially, Amtrak acquired the passenger rail operations of numerous private railroads, consolidating routes and resources under one entity. This move was crucial in preventing the complete dissolution of intercity rail travel in

America, which had become increasingly fragmented and unprofitable for individual companies.

Despite its ambitious beginnings, Amtrak faced numerous financial struggles from the onset. The funds allocated by the federal government were insufficient to cover the extensive costs required to overhaul aging infrastructure and modernize services. Rail lines, stations, and rolling stock were often in dire need of repair, leading to frequent delays and service interruptions. These operational hiccups only compounded Amtrak's financial woes, as they drove potential passengers away and further reduced revenue.

The mixed reactions from the public and state governments highlighted varying sentiments toward the necessity and viability of maintaining a robust passenger rail network. For some, Amtrak represented hope—an opportunity to preserve a vital piece of American heritage and a practical alternative to crowded highways and airports. Others viewed it skeptically, concerned about the substantial federal subsidies required to keep it afloat. Different states exhibited varied levels of enthusiasm and support, reflecting broader regional priorities and economic conditions. Places with stronger historical ties to rail travel or geographical constraints that favored train travel were more likely to support Amtrak's mission.

One of the critical challenges Amtrak confronted was that initial funding did not match the scale of the task at hand. Early financial troubles were exacerbated by the poor state of infrastructure inherited from failing private railroads. Tracks, signaling systems, and station facilities needed extensive upgrades and maintenance, which required significant capital investment. Without adequate funding, Amtrak struggled to offer reliable and attractive services, which in turn hampered its ability to draw passengers and generate income.

The financial trials and infrastructural deficiencies raised questions about the future of passenger rail services in a rapidly changing transportation landscape. However, over time, Amtrak managed to make incremental improvements, addressing some of the most glaring issues within its network. Federal assistance remained crucial, highlighting the importance of sustained government support for public transportation initiatives.

Public perception of Amtrak's value evolved as the organization made strides in stabilizing its operations. Initially met with skepticism, Amtrak gradually began to shift opinions about the practicality and necessity of government-backed rail services. In cities along successful routes, such as the Northeast Corridor, the utility of an efficient rail system became evident. Here, trains could compete favorably with both car and air travel, offering convenience and speed for intercity journeys.

Yet, the broader challenge was convincing the wider population of Amtrak's relevance in regions where rail wasn't historically entrenched or seen as vital. Marketing campaigns and community outreach programs aimed to highlight the benefits of rail travel, from environmental sustainability to congestion reduction on highways. While these efforts met with varying degrees of success, they did contribute to a gradual increase in awareness and appreciation of the role that passenger rail could play in the nation's transportation matrix.

Throughout these efforts, Amtrak's existence underscored a fundamental shift in perceptions regarding intercity rail travel. Unlike private railroads, which operated strictly on profit motives, Amtrak represented a model where government support was integral to ensuring the continuity of vital public services. This new framework suggested that rail travel, while perhaps not always immediately profitable, was worth preserving for its broader societal benefits. The emphasis on connectivity, both within and between states, was central to this philosophy.

This period also reflected broader trends in public transportation policy and urban planning. Government involvement in passenger rail suggested a recognition of the diverse needs of the population and the limitations of relying solely on road and air transport. Policymakers and urban planners began to see the potential of integrated, multi-modal transportation systems where rail played a key role alongside other forms of transit.

Cutbacks and Service Reductions

During the 1960s and 1970s, the American passenger rail service faced a period of significant financial strain, leading to considerable cuts and reductions. One of the most visible impacts of these austerity measures were the widespread route closures during the 1970s. Economic realities forced many rail companies to limit their services and abandon less profitable routes. Rail lines that once threaded through expansive rural landscapes and bustling urban centers were systematically pared back. This wave of closures starkly revealed the economic pressures squeezing the industry, ultimately shrinking the network and altering the transportation landscape of the nation.

In particular, the reduction in routes illuminated the disparity between urban and rural areas regarding service provision. City dwellers, despite some cuts, often retained access to essential rail services due to higher population densities and greater demand. Conversely, rural areas saw their already limited services slashed considerably, leaving sparsely populated regions more isolated than ever. The inequities in service provision became glaring, as rural communities found themselves marginalized, raising critical questions about equal access to transportation infrastructure.

Alongside the route closures, decreased funding for passenger rail services had immediate and long-lasting repercussions on the quality of travel. With fewer financial resources available, railway companies struggled to maintain their existing infrastructure. What followed was a noticeable decline in the physical condition of the tracks and stations, some of which had been architectural marvels and cultural landmarks in their heyday. The wear and tear on these structures went largely unaddressed, contributing to a gradual degradation in safety and reliability. Furthermore, passengers who relied on these trains began to experience diminished amenities, turning what was once considered an elegant mode of travel into a utilitarian and less comfortable journey. The allure of train travel dimmed, pushing potential passengers towards alternative modes of transportation such as automobiles and airlines, which appeared more convenient and appealing.

These cuts and reductions brought to the forefront enduring debates over the necessity and viability of sustained investment in rail infrastructure. Advocates for passenger rail argued that persistent underfunding and neglect perpetuated a vicious cycle: deteriorating services led to declining ridership, which further justified subsequent funding cuts. They emphasized that maintaining and improving passenger rail required consistent and substantial investment to reverse the downward trend. Meanwhile, opponents cited the mounting costs and perceived inefficiencies, advocating instead for channeling funds to other forms of transportation that seemed to promise better returns on investment. This debate highlighted the broader ideological divides regarding public transportation policy and fiscal priorities.

The story of the 1960s and 1970s passenger rail reveals much about the challenges faced by an industry caught in the crossfire of economic constraints and changing public preferences. Significant route closures during this era signaled not only a reaction to financial distress but also a deeper reevaluation of how transportation networks should be configured. Rural areas bore the brunt of these reductions, underscoring a critical issue of equity in public service provision. Declining funding translated directly into worsening infrastructure and service quality, making passenger rail less competitive with other transport options. Ultimately, these issues fueled ongoing discussions about the role of passenger rail in America's future and the importance of committing to its revival.

As rail lines withdrew from vast swathes of territory, the practical consequences for those dependent on train travel became increasingly apparent. For many Americans, particularly those in less affluent or more remote locations, the loss of passenger rail service meant sacrificing a crucial link to larger economic and social hubs. This reinforced existing socioeconomic disparities and highlighted the unequal impacts of transportation policy decisions. Urban centers often benefited from lobbying power and concentrated political influence, ensuring they maintained at least a skeleton service. In contrast, rural and less politically prominent areas suffered disproportionately from the cuts. This imbalance fed into wider discussions on the responsibilities of government and private corporations in providing equitable public services across diverse geographies.

Accompanying the contraction of the rail network was a tangible sense of nostalgia and loss among rail enthusiasts and everyday users alike. Train stations that had once teemed with life and activity slowly succumbed to decay. The romanticized image of rail travel, with its promise of leisurely yet efficient movement across picturesque landscapes, gave way to harsh reality. Dilapidated carriages, infrequent schedules, and subpar onboard conditions became the new norm. Passengers who continued to rely on trains found themselves dealing with increased delays, cancellations, and a general decline in overall travel experience. These negative experiences reinforced the perception that passenger rail was an outdated and impractical option, further driving down patronage in a self-reinforcing cycle.

Despite the profound difficulties, some voices remained steadfast in their belief in the potential of rail travel. They pointed to examples from other countries where sustained investment had yielded thriving and efficient railway systems. These international models served as case studies illustrating what could be achieved when commitment and resources were directed towards revitalizing passenger rail. However, in the U.S., bringing about such a renaissance required overcoming formidable obstacles, including entrenched interests favoring road and air transport, budgetary constraints, and a critical need to modernize aging infrastructure.

The discourse around passenger rail in this tumultuous period was emblematic of broader tensions within American society. It reflected struggles over the allocation of resources, the prioritization of different transport technologies, and visions for the future of mobility. As policymakers grappled with these issues, the consequences of underinvestment and service reduction became abundantly clear. They served as powerful reminders of what was at stake—whether an efficient, equitable, and sustainable transportation network could be realized, or whether the country would continue on a trajectory of fragmented and increasingly car-dependent mobility.

Public Perception Issues

In the 1960s and 70s, public perception of rail travel underwent significant transformation, largely driven by broader societal changes and specific events that influenced how people viewed train travel. One of the most impactful factors was the rise of automobiles and airplanes, which offered convenience and speed that trains struggled to compete with. As car ownership became more affordable and roads improved, people began to favor the autonomy and flexibility that driving provided. Similarly, commercial air travel grew in popularity, offering fast long-distance travel that trains could not match.

The shift towards automobiles and airlines wasn't just about convenience; it was also about a sense of modernity and progress. Cars and planes were seen as symbols of technological advancement and personal freedom, while trains began to represent an older, less dynamic form of travel. This perception was reinforced by the changing lifestyles of the era. Suburbanization meant that many people lived further away from train stations, making car travel more practical for daily commutes and errands.

Meanwhile, the burgeoning airline industry capitalized on this trend by marketing air travel as a glamorous and futuristic experience, further diminishing the allure of trains.

High-profile accidents during this period also played a critical role in shaping public confidence in rail safety. Incidents such as the tragic collision of two commuter trains in Darien, Connecticut, in 1969 drew widespread media attention, instilling fear and doubt among potential passengers. These accidents highlighted the vulnerabilities of the aging rail infrastructure and raised questions about maintenance standards and safety protocols. The emotional impact of these accidents cannot be underestimated; they not only claimed lives but also left lasting impressions on the public psyche, leading many to reconsider their travel choices.

In addition to safety concerns, ineffective marketing strategies by rail companies failed to attract new passengers or retain existing ones. During this era, marketing efforts often lacked coherence and failed to convey the unique advantages of train travel. While airlines boasted of their speed and cars were marketed for their convenience, rail companies struggled to find a compelling narrative. Advertising campaigns, when they existed, frequently focused on outdated notions of luxury that no longer resonated with contemporary travelers who were seeking efficiency and reliability.

Moreover, the competition wasn't just external; internal mismanagement and financial constraints within rail companies led to inconsistent service quality, which further eroded public trust. Passengers often faced delays, uncomfortable conditions, and poor customer service, experiences that did little to enhance the appeal of rail travel. In an era where other modes of transport were rapidly improving, these shortcomings were particularly glaring.

Media representations of rail travel during this time only exacerbated negative perceptions. Movies, television shows, and news reports frequently depicted trains as relics of a bygone era. This portrayal influenced public sentiment, creating a narrative that trains were outdated and inefficient compared to the sleek, modern alternatives of cars and planes. Popular culture's fascination with speed and innovation made trains seem like an antiquated choice, suitable perhaps for nostalgic journeys but not for practical, everyday use.

While trains had once been celebrated for their role in connecting communities and enabling economic growth, by the 1960s and 70s, they were increasingly seen as part of the past rather than the future. This shift in narrative was partly due to the failure of rail companies to innovate and adapt to changing consumer expectations. Unlike the automobile and airline industries, which continuously introduced new technologies and services, the rail industry lagged behind, further cementing the impression that it was out of touch with contemporary needs and desires.

However, it's important to note that these evolving perceptions were not uniform across all demographics. Some segments of the population continued to see value in rail travel, particularly those without access to cars or those who favored the environmental benefits of trains. Despite the challenges, there remained a dedicated group of rail enthusiasts and advocates who championed the cause of passenger rail services, recognizing their potential for sustainable transportation. This advocacy would later play a crucial role in efforts to revitalize and reshape the rail industry.

Notable Failures and Limited Successes

Efforts to revitalize passenger rail services during the 1960s and 1970s faced numerous challenges. Political and financial support was often inconsistent or insufficient, leading to a series of failed initiatives. For example, several private railroad companies attempted to revive their passenger services by introducing new luxury trains and modern amenities in hopes of attracting travelers away from growing competition such as airlines and automobiles. Despite these efforts, the lack of sustained funding and political backing meant many of these projects were short-lived. An example of this is the Santa Fe Railway's introduction of the "Super Chief" – a luxury passenger train that struggled to maintain profitability despite its high-quality service.

Conversely, certain regions managed to achieve localized successes. The Northeast Corridor, which runs from Boston through New York City to Washington, D.C., is a prime example. This area benefitted from higher population density, more substantial economic activity, and better political advocacy compared to other regions. Investments in infrastructure improvements, such as electrification and track upgrades, enabled more efficient and reliable services. The New Haven Railroad, for instance, saw an increase in ridership due to these enhancements, though financial struggles continued to plague the operations long-term.

The failures experienced in various revitalization attempts provided valuable lessons for future rail policy discussions. One critical lesson was the necessity for consistent and adequate funding. The sporadic financial support during the 1960s and 1970s highlighted that without a steady stream of investment, even promising initiatives could not sustain themselves. Moreover, political will played a significant role, as projects with strong government backing tended to fare better. The mixed success of state-supported rail services illustrated the importance of cohesive federal involvement alongside local efforts.

These historical attempts further emphasized the need for adaptive strategies in modern initiatives. Recognizing the specific causes of past failures, such as inadequate funding, political inconsistency, and competition from other modes of transport, modern planners and policymakers are better equipped to design sustainable solutions. For instance, current high-speed rail proposals often include comprehensive funding plans and robust political support mechanisms to avoid pitfalls encountered in earlier decades.

Reflecting on the broader historical context, it becomes evident that these revitalization attempts were not merely isolated incidents but part of a larger narrative of changing transportation habits and economic conditions. The post-war era saw a significant shift towards automobile ownership and air travel, driven by a combination of technological advances, economic prosperity, and changing lifestyle preferences. This societal shift made it increasingly challenging for rail services to compete, thereby necessitating innovative and resilient approaches to remain viable.

In addition, examining the specific corridors that achieved success provides insights into what factors contribute to effective rail service. High population densities and economic vitality in the Northeast

Corridor underline the importance of targeted investment in regions with the highest potential for ridership growth. These areas can then serve as models for developing similar initiatives in other parts of the country.

Overall, the attempts to revitalize passenger rail services during the 1960s and 1970s offer a rich tapestry of lessons and experiences. While many efforts were unsuccessful due to a complex interplay of political and financial challenges, the localized successes provide hope and direction for future endeavors. Understanding and applying these historical insights allows for more informed and strategic planning as modern society seeks sustainable and effective transportation solutions.

Final Thoughts

This chapter examined the various efforts to sustain passenger rail services during the 1960s and 1970s, highlighting the significant challenges and responses faced by an industry in decline. Federal policies initially favored automobile and air travel, diverting crucial funding away from rail services. Despite these setbacks, state-level interventions showed varied success in maintaining regional rail operations, with some areas like New York and California striving to keep commuter trains running. The introduction of

Amtrak marked a critical federal acknowledgment of the importance of passenger rail, though it initially struggled with financial and infrastructural hurdles. This era underscored the need for balanced investment and long-term strategies to preserve rail services amidst shifting transportation priorities.

Looking back, the policy decisions of the 1960s and 70s offer valuable insights into today's discussions on sustainable transportation. Issues such as environmental impact, economic disparities, and urban-rural connectivity remain central to current debates. The creation of Amtrak and state efforts to support regional rails highlight the complexities and necessities of coordinated government action in transportation planning. These historical endeavors demonstrate the ever-present challenge of securing consistent funding and political will to support public transit systems. As modern society continues to evolve, the lessons from this period serve as a guide for building a more resilient and efficient rail network that meets diverse needs and promotes sustainable development.

Chapter Five

Challenges Faced by Amtrak

A mtrak has faced significant challenges since its inception, particularly in operational and financial aspects that have hindered its ability to provide efficient passenger rail service. These challenges manifest in various forms, including stringent budget constraints and the persistent struggle with aging infrastructure. The budgetary limitations restrict Amtrak's capacity to maintain and expand its services, often resulting in service reductions and operational inefficiencies. This lack of consistent funding from federal subsidies further compounds these issues, making long-term planning difficult. Additionally, the high operating costs and low fare prices create a revenue model that is difficult to sustain, leading to deferred maintenance and periodic service reductions. Instances of financial mismanagement have only added to these burdens, highlighting the necessity for more effective resource management.

This chapter delves into the multiple layers of operational and financial hurdles that Amtrak has encountered over the years. It examines how historical underfunding has led to service cutbacks and a decline in service quality. The text also explores the role of federal subsidies and their inconsistency due to changing political priorities. Issues related to revenue generation, such as high operating costs and low fare prices, are scrutinized to understand their impact on Amtrak's financial health. Furthermore, the chapter addresses instances of financial mismanagement and emphasizes the importance of proper governance and accountability. By understanding these challenges, readers gain insight into the complex nature of running a national passenger rail service and the critical areas that need attention for future improvements.

Budget Constraints

Budget limitations have been a persistent challenge for Amtrak, deeply affecting its operations and long-term planning. The impacts of these financial constraints are multi-faceted, with historical underfunding at the forefront. Since its inception, Amtrak has struggled to secure adequate funding to maintain and expand its services. This lack of investment has resulted in service cutbacks and operational inefficiencies, which directly contribute to a decline in service quality. For instance, numerous scheduled routes have been canceled or reduced, disrupting travel plans for passengers and diminishing the reliability that is crucial for any transportation service.

In addition to historical underfunding, Federal subsidies play a critical role in Amtrak's financial stability. However, these subsidies are often inconsistent due to shifting political priorities. Changes in administration and differing views on public transportation funding lead to unpredictable budget allocations. This inconsistency creates a precarious financial situation for Amtrak, complicating its ability to plan for the future. Long-term projects and improvements are difficult to commit to when funding streams are uncertain. This volatility can force Amtrak to focus resources on short-term fixes rather than strategic growth and enhancement initiatives that would benefit passengers in the long run.

Revenue generation presents another significant hurdle for Amtrak. High operating costs combined with low fare prices mean that Amtrak struggles to achieve a sustainable revenue model. Unlike other transportation modes that may have more flexible pricing structures or alternative revenue streams, Amtrak's fare prices are often kept low to remain competitive and accessible. Unfortunately, this approach means that operational costs frequently outstrip revenue, leading to financial deficits. These shortfalls result in deferred maintenance and periodic service reductions. Deferred maintenance, in particular, exacerbates existing problems, as infrastructure continues to age without timely upgrades or repairs. The longer necessary maintenance is postponed, the costlier and more disruptive it becomes when it can no longer be ignored.

Compounding these issues are instances of financial mismanagement within Amtrak. There have been cases where poor financial decisions further strained already limited resources. Inefficient allocation of funds and lack of oversight can lead to wastage and suboptimal use of available money. Financial mismanagement underscores the importance of efficient resource management practices. Proper governance and accountability are essential in ensuring that every dollar is used effectively to enhance operations and improve service quality.

Maintenance and Aging Infrastructure

Amtrak's struggle with aging infrastructure and deferred maintenance has significantly escalated its operational challenges. The current state of Amtrak's trains and tracks presents considerable safety and reliability concerns. Over the years, the wear and tear on these assets have become increasingly evident, impacting their ability to deliver consistent and timely service. This degradation leads to frequent delays, which in turn affects public trust and confidence in the service.

Safety is another major concern tied to the outdated infrastructure. Many of the components such as bridges, tunnels, and tracks are well beyond their intended lifespan, raising the risk of accidents and other safety issues. These problems not only endanger passengers but also cast a shadow over Amtrak's reputation. Public trust erodes when passengers perceive that their safety is compromised, leading them to seek alternative modes of transportation.

Deferred maintenance is closely linked to budgetary restrictions, which further aggravates the situation. When essential repairs are delayed due to insufficient funding, minor issues often escalate into major problems requiring emergency interventions. This reactive approach to maintenance is significantly more costly compared to proactive upkeep. Emergency repairs disrupt schedules, causing operational delays that ripple through the entire network. Additionally, the costs associated with sudden fixes are much higher than planned maintenance, putting additional financial strain on an already stretched budget.

The backlog of repairs has grown so extensive that it creates a compounding effect. Each delay in maintenance increases the scope and cost of future repairs, creating a vicious cycle that is difficult to break. The longer assets remain unrepaired or inadequately maintained, the more unreliable they become, introducing further operational difficulties and compromising the overall service quality.

When comparing Amtrak's situation with competitors, it becomes apparent that better-maintained infrastructure in other transportation modes greatly enhances their reliability and customer satisfaction. For instance, many European rail systems place a high priority on regular maintenance and infrastructure upgrades, resulting in more dependable services. Similarly, airlines invest heavily in maintaining their fleet and support systems, ensuring minimal service disruptions. These competitors highlight the stark contrast in reliability and performance levels, revealing a critical area where Amtrak lags.

The superior performance of competing transportation modes underscores the importance of prioritizing infrastructure investment. Rail systems in countries like Japan and Germany have set high standards for efficiency and punctuality, thanks to their sustained focus on maintenance and technological upgrades. These systems illustrate how ongoing investment in infrastructure can create a seamless and reliable transportation experience, winning broader public approval and loyalty.

A strategic plan focused on addressing these issues must prioritize funding allocation towards infrastructure upgrades. One effective approach is to adopt proactive maintenance initiatives, drawing inspiration from successful examples worldwide. Proactive maintenance involves regularly scheduled inspections and timely addressing of small issues before they escalate into larger, more costly problems. By following this method, Amtrak can gradually reduce its backlog of deferred maintenance and improve operational reliability.

For instance, the implementation of advanced monitoring technologies can detect potential failures before they occur. These technologies enable predictive maintenance, allowing Amtrak to replace or repair components just as they begin to show signs of wear. This not only helps in preventing unexpected breakdowns but also optimizes the lifecycle of the assets, ensuring they remain functional and safe for a longer period.

Funding is crucial for these plans to materialize. Amtrak needs to secure stable and adequate financial resources to efficiently undertake the necessary infrastructure improvements. Collaborative efforts with federal and state governments, as well as exploring public-private partnerships, could provide the required funding. A dedicated approach towards securing these funds will be instrumental in facilitating the necessary upgrades.

Real-life examples demonstrate the benefits of proactive maintenance and strategic planning. For example, the Northeast Corridor (NEC) Improvement Project focused on upgrading critical segments of track and bridge replacements. Although progress has been slow due to funding constraints, the initiative has already shown promising results in terms of improved ride quality and reduced delays. Expanding such projects across the network can yield similar benefits, enhancing overall service reliability.

Furthermore, integrating sustainable practices within maintenance strategies can also play a significant role. Utilizing environmentally friendly materials and energy-efficient technologies can reduce the carbon footprint of maintenance activities, aligning with broader goals of sustainability and environmental stewardship.

Service Reliability Problems

Amtrak, the National Railroad Passenger Corporation, has faced a myriad of challenges since its inception, particularly in the realm of service reliability. This section delves into these ongoing issues and their multifaceted impact on ridership and public perception.

One of the most pressing concerns is Amtrak's on-time performance, which perpetually garners poor ratings. Statistics reveal that a significant portion of Amtrak's trains fail to meet scheduled arrival times. For example, in recent years, on-time performance figures have hovered around 75%, meaning one out of every four trains arrives late. Such statistics are crucial as they directly influence consumer confidence. When passengers cannot rely on timely travel, their trust in the service diminishes. Decreased consumer confidence inevitably leads to lower ridership numbers, posing a threat to Amtrak's competitive edge in the transportation market.

Several factors contribute to these service reliability issues. Weather-related disruptions are a frequent cause, with harsh winters, hurricanes, and other natural events leading to delays and cancellations. Infrastructure failures also play a significant role. For instance, track malfunctions, signal problems, and mechanical breakdowns are common occurrences that disrupt schedules. Additionally, external delays, such as those caused by freight train interference, further compound operational interruptions. These cumulative disruptions frustrate passengers, who often find themselves stranded or significantly delayed.

Passenger dissatisfaction is mirrored in customer experience surveys, which underscore the importance of punctuality and reliability. Survey results consistently highlight that passengers prioritize timely arrivals and departures. The negative feedback associated with delays not only tarnishes Amtrak's reputation but also impacts overall customer satisfaction. Passengers who experience frequent delays are less likely to use the service again, and negative word-of-mouth can deter potential new riders. In a world where online reviews and social media posts can spread rapidly, maintaining punctual service is more critical than ever for retaining and attracting customers.

To fully grasp the magnitude of Amtrak's service reliability issues, it is insightful to compare its performance with global rail carriers. For instance, Japan's Shinkansen bullet trains are renowned for their exceptional punctuality, boasting on-time performance rates of over 99%. Similarly, European rail services, such as those in Switzerland and Germany, consistently outperform Amtrak in terms of reliability. These comparisons reveal stark deficiencies in Amtrak's operations. While some differences can be attributed to variations in geography and funding, the operational practices of these global counterparts provide valuable lessons. Emphasizing preventive maintenance, investing in infrastructure upgrades, and adopting advanced scheduling technologies are strategies that could potentially enhance Amtrak's reliability.

Understanding these service reliability issues is crucial for addressing the broader implications on ridership and public perception. Amtrak's struggle with punctuality and dependability not only affects day-to-day operations but also its long-term viability as a preferred mode of transportation. Persistent delays hinder Amtrak's ability to attract business travelers, who often seek reliable and efficient travel options. Furthermore, leisure travelers, who may initially choose rail travel for its scenic routes and comfort, may turn away after experiencing repeated delays.

Infrastructure improvements are essential for resolving many of the service reliability issues. Upgrading tracks, signals, and train systems would reduce the frequency of mechanical failures and disruptions. Investments in better weather forecasting and response strategies can mitigate the impact of adverse weather conditions. Additionally, prioritizing passenger trains over freight trains on shared tracks could alleviate some of the external delays currently affecting Amtrak services. These changes require substantial financial resources, but the long-term benefits to service reliability, customer satisfaction, and ridership growth could justify the investment.

Internally, Amtrak must foster a culture focused on reliability and customer service. Training employees to handle disruptions effectively and communicate transparently with passengers can improve the travel experience, even when delays occur. Empowering staff to address passenger concerns promptly and satisfactorily ensures that customers feel valued and heard, which can help mitigate dissatisfaction stemming from service disruptions.

The comparative analysis with international rail carriers sheds light on several best practices that Amtrak could adopt. For instance, the integration of real-time monitoring systems for tracks and trains, as seen in high-performing rail networks, can preemptively identify issues before they result in delays. Collaboration with freight operators to develop mutually beneficial schedules can minimize interference and improve on-time performance. Learning from these international examples and tailoring solutions to fit the unique challenges faced by Amtrak could pave the way for enhanced service reliability.

Political Influences and Funding Issues

Political dynamics have long played a significant role in shaping the operational capacity and funding of

Amtrak. The changing landscape of political priorities, administration shifts, lobbying efforts, and the partnership, or lack thereof, with private entities profoundly influence the strategic direction of this vital passenger rail service.

Firstly, the fluctuations in political administrations and their respective priorities render Amtrak's budget allocations highly unpredictable. Each new administration comes with its own set of transportation policies, often leading to drastic changes in funding for Amtrak. For instance, one administration might prioritize infrastructure investment and allocate generous funds to modernize rail services, while another might shift focus to road transport, resulting in budget cuts. This volatility poses a significant challenge as it disrupts long-term planning and operational efficacy. Without a stable financial outlook, it becomes challenging for Amtrak to commit to multi-year projects or extensive modernization efforts, often resulting in deferred maintenance and an inability to upgrade equipment.

Lobbying and advocacy efforts are another critical aspect shaping Amtrak's funding and operational scope. Advocacy groups, industry stakeholders, and even regional politicians continually lobby for more substantial investment in passenger rail. These efforts aim to secure more predictable and increased funding from federal and state governments. However, the effectiveness of these lobbying efforts underscores the necessity of having a well-coordinated political strategy. For example, successful campaigns often hinge on presenting compelling evidence of Amtrak's economic impact, environmental benefits, and potential role in alleviating urban congestion. By capitalizing on these arguments, advocates can persuade policymakers to invest more significantly in rail infrastructure.

Guideline: To ensure effective lobbying and advocacy, Amtrak and its supporters need to develop a coordinated strategy that emphasizes the economic and environmental benefits of enhanced rail service. This strategy should include detailed impact studies, clear communication campaigns, and strong alliances with influential stakeholders.

The absence of robust public-private partnerships further restricts Amtrak's investment opportunities. Unlike other sectors where such collaborations have resulted in substantial improvements and financial stability, Amtrak has seen limited success in this area. Public-private partnerships (PPPs) can offer a model for how Amtrak might sustain itself financially while expanding and improving services. Successful examples from other countries demonstrate that involving private enterprises can bring innovative solutions, additional capital, and efficiency gains. For instance, Japan's railway system benefits significantly from private sector involvement, which helps maintain high standards of service and technological advancement. Replicating such models could provide Amtrak with much-needed financial injections and operational improvements.

Guideline: Establishing strategic public-private partnerships is essential for Amtrak. Potential steps include identifying feasible collaboration areas, engaging with prospective private partners through transparent processes, and developing mutually beneficial agreements that clearly outline roles, responsibilities, and profit-sharing mechanisms.

Moreover, current political influences pose future implications that cannot be ignored. The instability engendered by political uncertainties not only hampers present-day operations but also discourages long-term investments in modernization. Potential investors, whether governmental bodies or private entities, often seek a stable and predictable policy environment before committing substantial resources. When faced with fluctuating political support and accompanying financial unpredictability, they may opt to hold back, thereby stalling growth and service expansion plans. This hesitance directly impacts Amtrak's capacity to innovate and enhance the quality of its services, leaving it lagging behind international peers who operate within more stable frameworks.

Guideline: Addressing the future implications of political instability involves advocating for legislative measures that secure long-term funding commitments. Ensuring more consistent support requires developing bipartisan coalitions focused on the importance of rail transport for national infrastructure and economic health.

Customer Satisfaction and Service Quality

Customer satisfaction is a crucial metric that directly correlates with the quality of service provided by Amtrak. It encompasses a range of elements, from punctuality and cleanliness to staff behavior and overall comfort. A fundamental aspect of this relationship is the handling of customer complaints. When grievances are ignored or inadequately addressed, they contribute to attrition rates, eroding customer trust and loyalty. This attrition inevitably translates into diminished future revenues and lower ridership numbers as dissatisfied customers turn to alternative modes of transportation.

Quality control initiatives play a pivotal role in elevating the on-board experience for passengers. These initiatives often focus on comprehensive staff training programs designed to enhance customer interaction skills and improve service delivery. By implementing structured customer feedback mechanisms, Amtrak can continually refine its service standards. For instance, prompt adjustments based on passenger feedback can address recurring issues such as delays, cleanliness, and meal service quality. This proactive approach not only mitigates dissatisfaction but also fosters a sense of care and commitment in the eyes of the passengers, thereby increasing customer loyalty and repeat ridership.

Social media has become a powerful platform where public perception is shaped and shared instantaneously. Reviews and comments about Amtrak's service spread rapidly across various social networks, significantly impacting the company's reputation. Service failures, whether related to punctuality, cleanliness, or staff behavior, are quickly magnified through these channels. Negative reviews can deter potential passengers from choosing Amtrak, amplifying the urgency for immediate issue resolution. Conversely, positive experiences shared online can enhance Amtrak's image, attracting new riders and building a community of satisfied customers. Therefore, actively monitoring and responding to social media feedback is essential for maintaining and improving public perception.

Regular surveys and robust feedback mechanisms are instrumental in identifying specific areas for improvement within Amtrak's operations. These tools provide valuable insights into passengers' evolving expectations and preferences. By analyzing survey data, Amtrak can pinpoint persistent pain points such as delayed schedules, outdated amenities, or poor customer support, and devise targeted strategies to address them. Empirical evidence suggests that transportation providers who regularly solicit and act on passenger feedback tend to fare better in customer satisfaction ratings. Thus, staying attuned to customer voices not only enhances service quality but also aligns service offerings with current market demands.

Guidelines for effective quality control measures include involving front-line employees in the feedback process to ensure firsthand insights into operational challenges. Implementing regular training sessions that emphasize empathy, efficiency, and problem-solving can significantly uplift the quality of interactions between staff and passengers. Additionally, adopting cutting-edge technology for real-time feedback collection and analysis can streamline the process, enabling quicker and more accurate responses to customer needs.

Final Thoughts

The chapter delved into the significant operational and financial challenges that Amtrak has faced since its inception, highlighting how these issues have hampered its ability to provide reliable and efficient passenger rail service. Budget constraints, inconsistent federal subsidies, and high operating costs have led to service cutbacks and deferred maintenance, contributing to a decline in service quality and reliability. Additionally, financial mismanagement and aging infrastructure have compounded these problems, causing frequent delays and safety concerns that erode public trust and confidence in Amtrak's services.

Addressing these challenges requires a multifaceted approach focusing on securing stable funding, investing in infrastructure upgrades, and implementing proactive maintenance strategies. Learning from global counterparts, such as adopting advanced monitoring technologies and fostering public-private partnerships, could enhance Amtrak's operational efficiency and reliability. With a committed focus on improving infrastructure and financial stability, Amtrak can aspire to meet the high standards set by international rail systems, ultimately enhancing customer satisfaction and regaining public trust in its services.

Chapter Six

Routes That Work: Success Stories

S uccessful passenger rail routes in the U.S. provide invaluable insights into effective transportation planning and offer models for future initiatives. These routes illustrate how strategic investments, geographical advantages, governance structures, and sustainability efforts can create efficient, reliable, and attractive rail services. By examining these elements, we gain a deeper understanding of what makes certain rail systems thrive while others falter.

This chapter delves into several prominent examples of successful passenger rail routes across the country. It explores the Northeast Corridor's geographic benefits and continuous infrastructure investment, the Pacific Surfliner's scenic appeal and consistent scheduling, and Chicago's robust commuter rail integration and modern technology adoption. Additionally, it highlights emerging high-speed rail projects such as California's ambitious network and Texas Central Railway's private investment model. Each example not only illustrates success but also offers practical lessons for improving and expanding rail services nationwide.

Northeast Corridor

The Northeast Corridor (NEC) stands out as a model for successful passenger rail in the United States. Its geographic advantages, continuous investment in infrastructure, collaborative governance, and sustainability initiatives collectively define its success and serve as a blueprint for future rail projects.

First and foremost, the NEC benefits from significant geographic advantages. Stretching from Boston to Washington, D.C., it connects some of the most densely populated and economically vital urban centers in the country. This corridor encompasses major cities like New York, Philadelphia, and Baltimore, each contributing to high ridership levels. The proximity of these cities creates a natural demand for frequent and reliable train services, making it an essential transportation artery for both commuters and travelers. The ease with which passengers can travel between these urban centers makes rail travel an attractive alternative to driving or flying, especially given the often congested roadways and busy airports in the region.

Investing continuously in infrastructure has been crucial to the NEC's success. Modernizing tracks, upgrading signaling systems, and maintaining bridges and tunnels ensure that trains run efficiently and safely. For instance, the introduction of advanced train control systems has significantly reduced delays and improved overall punctuality. These investments not only enhance travel times but also contribute to safety, reinforcing the reliability of the service. A guideline for other rail projects is evident here: consistent and targeted investments in infrastructure are necessary to maintain and improve service quality. Future rail initiatives should prioritize funding for such enhancements to ensure long-term viability and safety.

Collaborative governance plays a pivotal role in the management and operation of the NEC. Unlike other rail networks managed by a single entity, the NEC benefits from the cooperative efforts of federal, state, and local authorities. This collaboration ensures that all stakeholders have a vested interest in the corridor's success. Effective communication and shared decision-making processes lead to more responsive and adaptable service improvements. As a guideline for other projects, fostering partnerships among various levels of government can result in better resource allocation, streamlined operations, and improved service quality.

Sustainability initiatives position the NEC as a leader in eco-friendly transportation. The shift towards electric trains, reducing carbon emissions, aligns with broader environmental goals. Additionally, projects promoting energy efficiency, such as regenerative braking systems and solar-powered stations, underscore the NEC's commitment to sustainability. This focus on green practices not only benefits the environment but also appeals to environmentally conscious passengers who prefer sustainable travel options. For other rail initiatives, adopting similar sustainability measures can help mitigate environmental impact while attracting a growing segment of eco-minded travelers.

California's Pacific Surfliner

The Pacific Surfliner stands as a model of effective regional rail service, recognized for its seamless blend of scenic travel and local connectivity. This line, which stretches along the Southern California coastline from San Luis Obispo to San Diego, offers passengers breathtaking coastal views that serve as a significant draw for leisure travelers. With its windows framing vistas of the Pacific Ocean, rolling hills, and picturesque beaches, the Pacific Surfliner provides an unparalleled travel experience that appeals to both tourists and residents seeking a comfortable and enjoyable journey.

One of the pivotal reasons behind the Pacific Surfliner's success is its consistent and reliable scheduling. Trains run frequently and on time, making it a dependable option for daily commuters as well as occasional travelers. This reliability builds trust among passengers, encouraging repeat patronage. It is crucial for any successful transit system to maintain a high level of punctuality, as delays can deter potential riders and compromise the overall reputation of the service. The Pacific Surfliner's adherence to its schedule plays a vital role in fostering a sense of dependability and convenience.

Another key factor contributing to the Pacific Surfliner's effectiveness is its integration with local transit systems. By connecting seamlessly with various regional buses, trolleys, and light rail services, the Surfliner enhances accessibility for passengers. This multi-modal approach allows travelers to navigate different parts of Southern California with ease, reducing the need for private vehicle use. Such integration not only improves the convenience for passengers but also supports broader goals of reducing traffic congestion and lowering environmental impacts.

The importance of this integrated network cannot be overstated. For example, a traveler landing at Los

Angeles International Airport (LAX) can take advantage of the FlyAway bus service to Union Station, where they can then board the Pacific Surfliner. This type of connectivity ensures that major transportation hubs are linked efficiently, making the rail service a more viable and attractive option for long-distance and local commutes alike. Furthermore, these connections often extend to smaller, less urbanized areas, thereby increasing ridership and expanding the service's reach across a diverse demographic landscape.

Sustainable funding models underpin the financial viability and continuous improvement of the Pacific Surfliner. Unlike some transportation networks that rely predominantly on public funding, the Surfliner employs a diversified approach. Funding streams include federal grants, state support, ticket revenues, and public-private partnerships. This multifaceted strategy not only ensures financial stability but also provides resources for upgrading infrastructure and enhancing passenger services. For instance, recent investments have led to the addition of new train cars with modern amenities, improving the overall travel experience.

These funding models also play a crucial role in maintaining fare affordability while still allowing for service enhancements. Public-private partnerships, in particular, bring in additional revenue and innovation from the private sector, fostering an environment of continuous improvement. Through strategic investments, the Pacific Surfliner can undertake projects such as track upgrades to increase speed, reduce travel times, and elevate safety standards. These efforts contribute to a better, more efficient service that meets the evolving needs of its user base.

A guideline for enhancing tourism appeal through scenic routes suggests leveraging natural landscapes and cultural landmarks to attract travelers. The Surfliner's route along the coast showcases stunning vistas and affords riders opportunities to relax and enjoy the scenery, turning a simple journey into an experiential adventure. Train travel enthusiasts and casual tourists alike appreciate the chance to see some of California's most beautiful coastal regions without the stress of driving or navigating crowded highways.

In terms of consistent scheduling, best practices emphasize robust operational planning and real-time monitoring to mitigate delays. The Pacific Surfliner's rigorous adherence to its timetable sets a standard for other rail services aiming to build a loyal customer base. Regular maintenance schedules and quick response teams for any disruptions ensure that trains run smoothly, reinforcing the reliability aspect that passengers rely on.

When it comes to community connections, creating a comprehensive transit ecosystem promotes higher ridership and regional development. Integrating various modes of transport, as seen with the Surfliner, maximizes accessibility and makes public transport a practical choice for a wider audience. Guidelines for successful integration highlight the necessity of coordinated schedules, shared ticketing systems, and strategic station locations to facilitate easy transfers between different types of transit.

Finally, guidelines for adopting diversified funding models advise combining traditional sources like government subsidies with innovative financing mechanisms. Examples include naming rights for stations, corporate sponsorships, and targeted service fees. Diversified funding not only enhances the service quality but also ensures long-term sustainability by spreading financial risks across multiple revenue streams.

Chicago-based Regional Services

The Chicago region has long been recognized as a beacon of effective rail service, seamlessly connecting its suburbs to the urban core. This accomplishment can be attributed to several key strategies that have made commuter rail an integral part of daily life for many residents.

Firstly, the extensive interconnectivity of routes in the Chicago area plays a significant role in maintaining robust rail services. The vast network of rails ensures that commuters from various suburbs can easily access the city center. This interconnected system reduces travel times and makes commuting more convenient. For instance, Metra, one of the primary commuter rail systems in the region, boasts 11 lines serving over 240 stations, which greatly facilitates the daily flow of commuters into the city. The strategic placement of these stations enables commuters from diverse neighborhoods to reach their destinations efficiently, minimizing the need for additional transit options.

Moreover, effective public relations campaigns are paramount in raising awareness and engagement among potential riders. The Metropolitan Rail Corporation (Metra) has consistently invested in public outreach initiatives to communicate the benefits of rail travel. Clear messaging regarding the convenience, cost savings, and environmental advantages of choosing rail over other forms of transportation has resonated with the public. Community events, social media campaigns, and partnerships with local businesses have further solidified the importance of rail travel within the collective consciousness of Chicago residents. To encourage public engagement, Metra has held informative sessions and open houses where passengers can learn about upcoming projects, service updates, and route changes.

Another crucial element contributing to the success of Chicago's rail services is the integration of modern technology. The adoption of advanced systems has significantly enhanced user experience and operational efficiency. For example, real-time tracking applications allow commuters to plan their journeys more effectively by providing up-to-date information on train schedules and delays. Additionally, the implementation of electronic ticketing options simplifies the purchasing process, making it more accessible even for those who may not regularly use rail services. These technological upgrades not only improve passenger satisfaction but also streamline operations for service providers, enabling them to address issues promptly and maintain high standards of service.

Guidelines are essential for the successful implementation of public relations and technology integration. For public relations, consistent communication with the community ensures that the message remains relevant and engaging. Collaborating with local media and utilizing diverse platforms can maximize outreach. For technology, ensuring user-friendly interfaces and regular updates keeps the system efficient and reliable.

Commuter comfort is another priority that the Chicago rail region addresses meticulously.

Recognizing that a pleasant travel experience can lead to increased ridership, Metra has focused on creating a comfortable environment for passengers. This includes investing in well-maintained, clean, and climate-controlled cars, ample seating, and onboard amenities such as Wi-Fi and power outlets. Stations are designed to be accessible and offer conveniences such as waiting areas, restrooms, and retail options. By focusing on these details, Metra encourages loyalty among its riders, who come to rely on the rail service for their daily commutes, knowing they can expect a comfortable and hassle-free journey.

The emphasis on commuter comfort is backed by regular surveys and feedback mechanisms that allow passengers to voice their experiences and suggestions. These insights are invaluable for continuous improvement and ensure that the services evolve according to passenger needs. Metra's dedication to enhancing commuter comfort stands as a testament to its commitment to providing exceptional rail services.

Emerging High-Speed Rail Projects

California's High-Speed Rail project offers a glimpse into what future rail initiatives could look like in the United States. This ambitious endeavor aims to connect major metropolitan areas such as San Francisco and Los Angeles, reshaping transportation across vast distances. By bridging these major hubs, the project highlights the importance of making travel between big cities more efficient, reducing both travel time and environmental impact.

The success of the California High-Speed Rail lies in its strategic alignment with economic centers. The route was meticulously planned to serve densely populated regions where the demand for rapid transit is high. This ensures that the rail line will not only be well-used but also financially viable. Additionally, it demonstrates how infrastructure investments can stimulate economic growth in connected areas, offering lessons for other states considering similar projects.

Private investment plays a crucial role in rail networks, as illustrated by the Texas Central Railway. This high-speed rail project plans to link Dallas and Houston using Japanese Shinkansen N700 technology. Unlike many public transportation projects that rely solely on government funding, Texas Central Railway leverages private funds to cover development costs. This model demonstrates how private sector involvement can expedite project timelines and reduce the financial burden on taxpayers.

The ability of private investors to inject capital into large-scale infrastructure projects shows a pathway for other states to follow. By attracting private stakeholders through promising returns on investment, high-speed rail projects can gain momentum and public support. Moreover, this approach emphasizes the need for clear, transparent partnerships between government entities and private companies to ensure mutual benefits and project success.

Looking globally, the success stories of the French TGV and Japanese Shinkansen provide practical design ideas for American high-speed rail. Both systems are renowned for their punctuality, speed, and efficiency, setting benchmarks for high-speed rail worldwide. For instance, the TGV has been a trailblazer in network expansion and technological advancements, while the Shinkansen is celebrated for its safety record and operational precision.

Adopting best practices from these international models can greatly benefit U.S. rail initiatives. From the rolling stock technology to the intricacies of station design and passenger services, these elements can be customized to fit American needs. Learning from global leaders allows U.S. projects to bypass some of the developmental challenges encountered by pioneers and implement tried-and-tested solutions directly into their planning and execution phases.

Addressing challenges is an integral part of any large-scale transportation project. Legislative battles and community engagement present significant hurdles that must be navigated thoughtfully. One of the first steps is garnering political support at local, state, and federal levels. Without broad legislative backing, even the most compelling high-speed rail proposals can stall indefinitely. Successful lobbying efforts and strategic alliances with influential policymakers can help secure necessary funding and regulatory approvals.

Community engagement is equally essential, as buy-in from local populations can make or break a project. Engaging with the community involves transparency about potential impacts and benefits, addressing concerns proactively, and incorporating public feedback into project planning. For instance, thorough environmental impact assessments and noise mitigation strategies can alleviate local opposition, while educational campaigns can build public enthusiasm for the benefits of high-speed rail.

Another persistent challenge is securing right-of-way access. Negotiating land acquisition in densely populated or privately owned areas often leads to legal disputes and project delays. Effective negotiation strategies, coupled with fair compensation for affected landowners, can streamline the process. Utilizing existing transportation corridors whenever possible can also minimize disruption and resistance.

Finally, inter-agency coordination remains key. High-speed rail projects typically require collaboration across multiple governmental departments, from transportation and urban planning to environmental protection agencies. Ensuring that all parties work cohesively towards common goals can prevent bureaucratic gridlock and facilitate smoother project progression.

Factors Contributing to Their Success

When examining the most successful passenger rail routes in the U.S., several common elements emerge as foundational to their success. These elements provide critical insights for policymakers, urban planners, and transportation enthusiasts who seek to enhance existing rail services or develop new ones.

The first element is strategic location combined with rigorous demand analysis. Successful rail routes are often strategically situated to serve densely populated areas with significant travel demand. For instance, routes that connect major metropolitan regions, such as those between New York, Washington D.C., and Boston, benefit from high ridership due to the sheer volume of daily commuters and travelers. Detailed demand analysis ensures that these routes are not only utilized but optimized for maximum efficiency and profitability. This involves studying population density, travel patterns, and economic activities, leading to informed decisions about route placement and service frequency. Such analysis can reveal underserved areas where new routes might thrive, or adjustments needed in existing services to better meet rider needs.

Public support and funding play pivotal roles in sustaining successful passenger rail routes. Without consistent financial backing, even well-planned routes can falter. Public support often manifests through community engagement, public awareness campaigns, and advocacy for rail services. When communities rally behind these initiatives, securing government funding and private investment becomes more feasible. Government grants, subsidies, and partnerships with private entities provide the capital necessary for infrastructure development, maintenance, and technological improvements. A clear guideline for ensuring public support includes engaging stakeholders early in the planning process, maintaining transparent communication, and demonstrating the tangible benefits of the railway system to the local economy and environment. Developing a strong case for funding based on projected economic growth, job creation, and environmental benefits can also be instrumental in winning over policymakers and potential investors.

Flexible operation models are another cornerstone of successful rail systems. The ability to adapt operations to changing demographics and consumer preferences is crucial. For example, incorporating varying ticket pricing structures to accommodate different income levels, offering diverse scheduling options to cater to both regular commuters and occasional travelers, and integrating modern conveniences such as Wi-Fi and comfortable seating can significantly enhance ridership. Rail operators need to stay attuned to demographic shifts, such as increases in urban populations or changes in work patterns, which might affect peak travel times. A flexible approach also involves adjusting service offerings based on feedback and performance data, ensuring that the rail service remains relevant and appealing to a broad user base.

Continual commitment to improvement guarantees long-term viability and passenger satisfaction. Successful rail operators invest in ongoing enhancements to infrastructure, technology, and customer service. This may involve upgrading tracks and stations, implementing advanced safety features, and adopting innovations such as real-time tracking and mobile ticketing. Regular assessments and updates ensure that the rail service meets contemporary standards and expectations. Monitoring customer feedback and conducting periodic reviews of operational efficiencies allow for the identification and rectification of issues before they become significant problems. A guideline here would suggest setting up a robust feedback mechanism, regularly investing in staff training, and staying ahead of industry trends to maintain a competitive edge.

Final Thoughts

As we have seen, successful passenger rail routes in the U.S. share several common elements that contribute to their effectiveness. These include strategic location with high population density, continuous infrastructure investment, collaborative governance, and a focus on sustainability. The Northeast Corridor exemplifies these principles by linking major urban centers, maintaining modernized infrastructure, and integrating green practices. Similarly, California's Pacific Surfliner benefits from its scenic route along the coastline, reliable scheduling, and integration with local transit systems. Moreover, Chicago's regional services thrive due to robust interconnectivity, effective public relations, and technological upgrades.

Emerging high-speed rail projects like those in California and Texas demonstrate the potential for future expansion of passenger rail in the U.S. Aligning these projects with economic centers ensures demand and financial viability, while private investments can accelerate development. Learning from global high-speed rail models such as the French TGV and Japanese Shinkansen can provide valuable insights for design and operation. Addressing challenges through political support, community engagement, and coordinated efforts across agencies will be essential. By adopting these lessons, future rail initiatives can contribute significantly to sustainable transportation solutions and enhanced connectivity across the country.

Chapter Seven

International Case Study: Japan's Shinkansen

J apan's Shinkansen, also known as the bullet train, represents a marvel of modern rail transport and engineering. Launched just before the Tokyo Olympics in 1964, the Shinkansen symbolized Japan's resurgence after World War II through its groundbreaking speed, efficiency, and technological innovation. This chapter takes a closer look at the historical context surrounding the Shinkansen's inception, exploring how it not only transformed transportation in Japan but also became a beacon of national pride and technological prowess. By examining the origins of this high-speed system within the framework of post-war reconstruction, readers will gain insight into the strategic vision that drove Japan to invest heavily in such an ambitious project.

Additionally, the chapter delves into various aspects that contribute to the Shinkansen's continued success. Topics include its pioneering design philosophy, which emphasizes aerodynamics and passenger comfort, and its responsiveness to challenges posed by natural disasters like earthquakes. The narrative will also cover the ways the Shinkansen has expanded over the decades, incorporating new technologies and innovations to stay ahead in the field of high-speed rail. Furthermore, the chapter highlights the Shinkansen's broader social and economic impacts, from boosting regional development and tourism to influencing rail systems worldwide. This comprehensive analysis aims to provide a nuanced understanding of why Japan's Shinkansen remains a model for successful high-speed rail systems globally.

Historical Background

The inauguration of Japan's Shinkansen, also known as the bullet train, in 1964 stands as a landmark event in both Japanese history and the evolution of rail transport. The Shinkansen began its operations on October 1st, 1964, just days before the Tokyo Olympics. This timing was not coincidental but strategic, showcasing Japan's resurgence on the world stage after World War II through technological prowess and innovation in transportation. The bullet train was emblematic of modernity, efficiency, and speed, capturing global attention and marking a significant technological milestone.

The inception of the Shinkansen came at a critical juncture during Japan's post-war reconstruction. In the years following World War II, Japan faced the daunting task of rebuilding its shattered economy and infrastructure. The government played a proactive role in spearheading large-scale infrastructure projects to stimulate economic recovery and modernization. Among these projects, the development of the Shinkansen was particularly notable. It wasn't merely about constructing a high-speed rail system; it represented a broader vision of advancement and progress that would contribute significantly to the country's rapid economic growth. With dedicated investment and planning, the Shinkansen became a symbol of national pride and economic resurgence.

The early design philosophy of the Shinkansen reflected an emphasis on modernity and efficiency. Engineers designed the trains with sleek, aerodynamic shapes to reduce air resistance and increase speed. The interiors were crafted to offer comfort and convenience to passengers, setting new standards for rail travel. This focus on design extended beyond functionality to embody the aspirations of a nation looking to redefine itself in the post-war era. Each element of the Shinkansen was carefully considered to project an image of technological excellence and forward-thinking ingenuity. This commitment to cutting-edge design has continued to influence rail systems around the world, establishing benchmarks that future high-speed trains aspire to meet.

Moreover, the adaptability and resilience of the Shinkansen have been demonstrated through various extensions, technology upgrades, and responses to natural disasters. Over the decades, the Shinkansen network has expanded significantly, connecting more regions and cities across Japan. These expansions were not just about increasing reach but also involved incorporating new technologies and innovations to enhance performance and passenger experience. For instance, technological upgrades over the years have improved speed, safety, and energy efficiency, keeping the Shinkansen at the forefront of high-speed rail technology.

In terms of resilience, the Shinkansen has shown remarkable robustness in responding to natural disasters such as earthquakes. Japan is prone to seismic activity, and ensuring the safety of the bullet train has always been a priority. Advanced earthquake detection systems have been implemented to automatically halt the trains in the event of seismic disturbances, significantly reducing risks to passengers. This ability to adapt and evolve in response to challenges has solidified the Shinkansen's reputation as a reliable and secure mode of transportation.

Another noteworthy aspect of the Shinkansen's success is the role it played in Japan's cultural narrative. As a product of post-war innovation and ambition, the Shinkansen became a point of national pride. It wasn't just a train but a symbol of what Japan could achieve through determination and technological advancement. This cultural significance is reflected in how the Shinkansen has been integrated into daily life and society. It has fundamentally changed the way people travel, work, and live, making long-distance commuting feasible and convenient. By connecting major urban centers with rural areas, the Shinkansen has also facilitated regional development and economic integration.

Furthermore, the Shinkansen has set global standards for other countries looking to develop their own high-speed rail systems. Its success has inspired similar projects worldwide, demonstrating the feasibility and advantages of high-speed rail networks. Countries such as France, China, and Spain have looked to Japan's model when designing their own systems, adopting many of the principles that made the Shinkansen successful. This influence underscores the global impact of the Shinkansen and its role in advancing rail technology.

Technological Advancements

The Shinkansen bullet train system stands as a
paragon of modern rail technology, renowned for its
remarkable efficiency, speed, and safety. One of the
critical factors contributing to this success is track
segregation. By dedicating specific tracks solely for
high-speed trains, the Shinkansen system minimizes
interference from slower, conventional trains. This
strategic separation not only increases operational
efficiency but also significantly boosts average speeds,
allowing the Shinkansen to maintain its impressive
schedule with minimal delays. Enhanced
aerodynamics further amplify these benefits. The
streamlined design of both the trains and the tracks
reduces air resistance, enabling faster travel and
improved fuel efficiency.

Another cornerstone of the Shinkansen's prowess lies
in its automated signaling systems. These systems
monitor the train operations in real-time, ensuring
that each train adheres to its schedule with pinpoint
accuracy. The integration of artificial intelligence (AI)
plays a crucial role here. AI algorithms analyze vast
amounts of data collected from various sensors along
the track and onboard the trains. This data-driven
approach allows for dynamic adjustments in train
operations, optimizing speed and maintaining safe
distances between trains. As a result, the Shinkansen
boasts an unparalleled record of punctuality, with

delays typically measured in mere seconds rather than minutes or hours.

Safety is paramount in any transportation system, and the Shinkansen exemplifies this through its dedicated focus on innovative technologies. Earthquake detection and avoidance systems are integral to the Shinkansen's safety infrastructure. Japan's frequent seismic activity necessitates such advanced measures. Sensors placed along the Shinkansen routes can detect even minor tremors, triggering automatic emergency braking systems to halt trains before larger earthquakes strike. This proactive approach has saved countless lives and serves as a model for other countries prone to seismic events.

In densely populated areas, noise pollution is a significant concern. The Shinkansen addresses this issue through sound-dampening designs. Engineers have developed specialized materials and structural modifications to minimize noise levels as the trains pass through urban areas. These designs include quieter wheels, smoother track surfaces, and barriers that absorb and deflect sound waves. This thoughtful consideration ensures that the progress brought about by high-speed rail does not come at the expense of residents' quality of life. Balancing technological advancements with environmental and societal responsibilities showcases the holistic approach taken by those behind the Shinkansen's development.

Beyond physical innovations, the cultural acceptance of the Shinkansen is noteworthy. In Japanese society, the train is more than just a mode of transport; it symbolizes progress and efficiency. The meticulous attention to detail in every aspect of the Shinkansen's operation reflects broader cultural values of precision and responsibility. This cultural resonance has fostered widespread public support and pride, further driving continuous improvements and innovations within the system.

Real-world applications of these technologies extend beyond Japan's borders. Countries around the world seek to emulate the Shinkansen's success, studying its technological framework and operational strategies. From track design to signaling systems, the Shinkansen provides a comprehensive blueprint for developing high-speed rail in various geographical and societal contexts. Policymakers and urban planners can draw valuable lessons from Japan's example, tailoring them to fit their unique needs and challenges.

Moreover, the Shinkansen's commitment to environmental sustainability cannot be overlooked. High-speed rail presents a greener alternative to air and road travel, reducing carbon emissions and reliance on fossil fuels. The energy-efficient design of the Shinkansen trains, combined with Japan's forward-thinking energy policies, makes the system not only a marvel of engineering but also a testament to sustainable development. As the world grapples with climate change, the Shinkansen offers a viable path towards reducing the environmental impact of mass transit.

Passenger comfort and convenience are also prioritized in the Shinkansen's design. Spacious seating, smooth rides, and reliable services enhance the travel experience, making high-speed rail a preferred choice for many. The emphasis on customer satisfaction aligns with broader trends in modern transportation, where user experience is becoming increasingly important. By setting high standards in these areas, the Shinkansen continues to lead by example, encouraging other rail systems to follow suit.

The story of the Shinkansen is one of relentless innovation and adaptation. From its inception over half a century ago to its current status as a global icon of high-speed rail, the Shinkansen has continually evolved to meet emerging challenges and opportunities. Its technological advancements, coupled with a deep-rooted commitment to safety and sustainability, ensure that the Shinkansen remains at the forefront of railway engineering.

Operational Efficiency

Japan's Shinkansen, also known as the bullet train, stands as a model of punctuality and customer satisfaction in high-speed rail systems. One key factor that contributes to its success is its precise and frequent scheduling system. The Shinkansen trains operate on a tightly controlled timetable, with departures often scheduled just minutes apart. This high frequency minimizes wait times for passengers and ensures that demand is met effectively, especially during peak hours. The meticulous planning behind these schedules involves sophisticated algorithms and real-time data analysis, allowing the system to adjust to fluctuations in demand seamlessly. Passengers benefit from reduced waiting times and the assurance of timely arrivals and departures.

Another pillar of the Shinkansen's operational excellence is the rigorous training programs for conductors and staff. Every member of the team undergoes comprehensive training that not only covers technical aspects but also emphasizes customer service. Staff are trained to embody the traditional Japanese values of respect and professionalism, ensuring that every passenger interaction is pleasant and courteous. For example, conductors are taught to bow to passengers when entering and leaving carriages, a gesture that reflects the respect ingrained in Japanese culture.

Furthermore, ongoing training programs keep staff updated on the latest safety protocols and technological advancements, maintaining a high standard of service.

In addition to training, the Shinkansen adopts a proactive approach to maintenance. Regular and thorough maintenance checks are a cornerstone of its operation, preventing potential issues before they arise. Advanced technologies, such as predictive maintenance systems, are employed to monitor the condition of trains and tracks continuously. These systems use sensors and data analytics to detect early signs of wear and tear or mechanical problems, allowing maintenance crews to address them promptly. This proactive strategy not only ensures the longevity of assets but also minimizes service interruptions, contributing to the overall reliability of the Shinkansen.

Real-time technology further enhances the passenger experience by providing up-to-date information. Digital displays and mobile applications deliver real-time updates on train schedules, delays, and platform changes, keeping passengers informed throughout their journey. This transparency helps passengers plan their travel more effectively and reduces the anxiety associated with unexpected changes. Additionally, the system's ability to provide real-time information about connecting services and local transport options adds another layer of convenience, making the entire travel experience smoother and more predictable.

Illustrating these practices with examples highlights their effectiveness. For instance, during the busy holiday seasons, the Shinkansen's precise scheduling allows it to handle increased passenger loads without compromising punctuality. The New Year period, known as "Shogatsu," sees millions of people traveling across Japan. Despite this surge, the Shinkansen maintains its renowned on-time performance, demonstrating the strength of its scheduling system. Similarly, the rigorous training of staff is evident in their quick and efficient handling of passenger inquiries and assistance, even during peak travel times.

The maintenance protocols of the Shinkansen are equally impressive. In 2018, for example, a small crack was discovered in an axle during a routine inspection. Thanks to the advanced monitoring systems in place, the issue was detected before it could cause any significant disruption. The affected train was swiftly taken out of service, and repairs were carried out with minimal impact on the overall schedule. This incident underscores the importance of proactive maintenance in ensuring the safety and reliability of the Shinkansen.

The implementation of real-time passenger information systems also provides substantial benefits. During the Typhoon Hagibis in 2019, many transportation networks in Japan faced severe disruptions. However, the Shinkansen's real-time information system allowed it to communicate effectively with passengers, providing timely updates on schedule changes and alternative arrangements. This level of communication helped manage passenger expectations and reduced confusion during a period of uncertainty.

These operational practices not only enhance the efficiency and reliability of the Shinkansen but also contribute significantly to passenger satisfaction. The combination of precise scheduling, well-trained staff, proactive maintenance, and real-time information creates a seamless travel experience that other high-speed rail systems can aspire to replicate. By prioritizing punctuality and customer experience, the Shinkansen sets a high standard in the world of high-speed rail.

For other rail networks seeking to improve their operations, adopting similar strategies could yield positive results. Implementing frequent scheduling systems tailored to passenger demand can enhance efficiency and reduce wait times. Investing in the continuous training of staff ensures a high level of customer service and adaptability to new technologies and procedures. Proactive maintenance, supported by advanced monitoring tools, can prevent service interruptions and extend the lifespan of rail assets. Lastly, integrating real-time information systems can improve transparency and passenger confidence, particularly during unforeseen disruptions.

Economic Impacts

The Shinkansen, Japan's high-speed bullet train, serves as a remarkable model of economic impact on society. Its inception not only transformed transportation but also acted as a significant catalyst for employment growth across various sectors. As construction and expansion of the Shinkansen network required extensive manpower, it spurred job creation in engineering, construction, and manufacturing. This employment boom extended beyond the immediate project, influencing industries such as hospitality, retail, and services along the rail lines. The ripple effect was substantial: local economies experienced revitalization and increased prosperity due to the influx of workers and subsequent consumer spending.

Examining cities with direct access to the Shinkansen, we see profound examples of urban rejuvenation. Take, for instance, the city of Kanazawa. Once relatively isolated, Kanazawa's integration into the Shinkansen network rapidly boosted its accessibility. This newfound connectivity attracted businesses and tourists, infusing the local economy with new energy. Real estate values surged, prompting investment in infrastructure and public amenities. Similarly, Nagoya witnessed significant urban development, transforming it into a bustling metropolis. The strategic placement of Shinkansen stations facilitated efficient commuting, encouraging sustainable urban planning that emphasized mixed-use developments and minimized urban sprawl. These case studies underline how high-speed rail systems can serve as linchpins in regional development strategies.

Tourism has seen a dramatic uptick thanks to the Shinkansen. Domestic travel within Japan became more convenient and time-efficient, making weekend getaways and intercity travel more feasible for residents. For international visitors, the Shinkansen epitomized efficiency and reliability, enhancing Japan's appeal as a travel destination. The increased ease of movement encouraged tourists to explore regions beyond the usual hotspots like Tokyo and Kyoto. Cities such as Hiroshima and Fukuoka became accessible day-trip options, enriching the tourist experience and spreading economic benefits more evenly across the country. Furthermore, tourism-related businesses, including hotels, restaurants, and local attractions, thrived under the consistent influx of visitors, contributing significantly to their respective local economies.

From an investment perspective, both public and private returns have been noteworthy. Public investment in the Shinkansen infrastructure showcased forward-thinking governance prioritizing long-term national benefits. The initial outlay for the development of the network was substantial, yet the returns have proven lucrative. Revenues generated through ticket sales, advertising, and ancillary services provided a steady income stream. Additionally, taxes from businesses and increased employment further bolstered government finances. On the private side, companies involved in the construction, maintenance, and operation of the Shinkansen reported healthy profits, affirming the financial viability of such large-scale infrastructure projects.

Investment returns are not limited to direct financial gains. There are broader economic implications, including enhanced productivity and competitiveness. The Shinkansen reduced travel time drastically, fostering business activity by enabling executives and employees to commute efficiently between cities. This operational efficiency translated into higher productivity levels and facilitated collaboration and innovation. Moreover, the Shinkansen established Japan's reputation as a leader in high-speed rail technology, opening avenues for exporting expertise and gaining international contracts for similar projects.

Peter Wretzky

Cultural Acceptance and Popularity

The evolution of transportation in Japan has undergone significant transformations, especially with the introduction of the Shinkansen bullet train. This technological marvel isn't just a means of travel but a symbol of national pride and cultural integration. The cultural embrace of the Shinkansen reveals much about Japanese society's values and priorities.

Historically, Japan has seen various trends that show a preference for public transportation over private modes. Several factors contribute to this trend, including geographic constraints, population density, and urban planning. Public transportation systems have always enjoyed support due to their efficiency and cost-effectiveness. However, the advent of the Shinkansen brought an unprecedented sense of national pride. Introduced in 1964, coinciding with the Tokyo Olympics, the Shinkansen quickly became more than just a train; it was a testament to Japan's technological prowess and resilience. It marked Japan's recovery from the devastation of World War II and its emergence as a global leader in innovation.

This national pride translated into widespread acceptance and admiration for the Shinkansen across different strata of society. Rail travel has become a fundamental part of daily life for millions of Japanese citizens. With trains running punctually and frequently, many people rely on them for commuting, business trips, and leisure travel. This integration into daily routines underscores the reliability and convenience offered by the Shinkansen system. Its influence extends beyond mere transportation; it affects social behavior and business practices. For instance, the ease of inter-city travel has fostered business relationships and partnerships across regions. Meetings and collaborations that once required extensive planning can now be executed seamlessly, thanks to the rapid connectivity provided by the Shinkansen.

Moreover, environmentally conscious travel is another significant aspect that has permeated Japanese culture through the use of the Shinkansen. High-speed rail is a cleaner alternative to air and road travel, reducing carbon emissions drastically. The Japanese government's initiatives to promote eco-friendly practices align well with the public's increasing awareness of environmental issues. These efforts have only added to the appeal of the Shinkansen as a preferred mode of transport.

An important element in fostering long-term usage and community engagement around the Shinkansen has been educational initiatives. Various programs aim to educate citizens about rail technology and its myriad benefits. Schools often include trips and lessons focused on the science behind high-speed rail, emphasizing its importance in modern society. Museums dedicated to rail history and technology attract both locals and tourists, serving as educational hubs. Such efforts ensure that the younger generation understands the value of this technology, helping to secure its continued popularity and utility. Guidelines for these educational initiatives often include partnerships with local schools, interactive exhibits, and hands-on activities that make learning about the Shinkansen fun and engaging for all ages.

Beyond its practical applications, the Shinkansen holds a unique place in Japanese art and literature. It frequently appears in various forms of media, from manga and anime to novels and films, reflecting its deep-rooted significance in Japanese culture. Artists depict the sleek, futuristic design of the Shinkansen, highlighting its role as a symbol of progress and modernity. Literature often uses it as a setting or metaphor, exploring themes of speed, change, and connectivity. This representation in art and media solidifies the Shinkansen's status as more than just a functional object; it becomes a cultural icon. Its portrayal ranges from the romantic to the philosophical, allowing the Shinkansen to resonate on multiple levels with audiences both within and outside Japan.

The Shinkansen's iconic status also contributes to international interest and tourism. Visitors often take trips on these famous trains to experience firsthand what they've read or seen in popular media. This influx of foreign tourists brings economic benefits and helps spread Japanese culture globally. The Shinkansen becomes a bridge connecting not only places but also people and cultures.

Final Insights

The chapter has explored the Shinkansen bullet train system as a model for successful high-speed rail. By delving into its historical background, technological advancements, operational efficiency, economic impacts, and cultural acceptance, we have seen how the Shinkansen represents more than just a mode of transport. It embodies Japan's post-war recovery, modern engineering prowess, and commitment to sustainability. The Shinkansen's design, punctuality, safety measures, and integration into daily life set a high standard that other countries aspire to achieve. This comprehensive analysis highlights the multifaceted benefits of high-speed rail, providing valuable insights for transportation enthusiasts, policymakers, urban planners, and academic scholars.

Moving forward, the lessons learned from the Shinkansen can inform future developments in global high-speed rail systems. Its success underscores the importance of strategic planning, continuous innovation, and cultural integration. As countries worldwide seek efficient, sustainable transportation solutions, Japan's experience serves as an exemplary guide. The Shinkansen's impact on urban development, economic growth, and environmental sustainability illustrates how well-executed infrastructure projects can transform societies. By adopting similar principles and addressing unique local challenges, regions across the globe can enhance connectivity, boost economic activity, and promote greener travel alternatives.

Chapter Eight

European Excellence: High-Speed Networks

High-speed rail networks in Europe exhibit remarkable achievements that have redefined the landscape of modern transportation. Among the standout examples are France's TGV, Germany's ICE, and Spain's AVE systems. These high-speed trains not only symbolize national pride and technological prowess but also illustrate the concerted efforts made by these countries to enhance connectivity and promote sustainable transport solutions. High-speed rail in Europe is a testament to innovation, strategic investment, and cross-border cooperation, offering valuable insights into how advanced rail systems can transform travel and economic dynamics.

In this chapter, we delve into the successful development and operational models of Europe's leading high-speed rail networks. By examining key case studies such as the TGV, ICE, and AVE, we will explore their inception, infrastructure, economic impacts, and passenger experience enhancements. Furthermore, we will look at the collaborative efforts across different European countries that foster interoperability and seamless travel between nations. Through these case studies, this chapter aims to provide a comprehensive understanding of the factors contributing to the efficiency and popularity of high-speed rail travel in Europe, offering lessons that could be applied globally.

France's TGV

The Train à Grande Vitesse, widely known as the TGV, stands as a testament to innovation in high-speed rail travel. Its inception came about as a response to increasing congestion on conventional railway lines and highways, coupled with a pressing need for rapid transport solutions. During the late 1960s and early 1970s, France faced significant challenges linked to urbanization and rising traffic volumes. Conventional railways were rendered inadequate for addressing the growing transportation demands, leading to delays and inefficiencies. It was within this context that the concept of the TGV emerged, aiming to provide a faster, more reliable alternative.

The introduction of dedicated tracks played a pivotal role in facilitating the unprecedented speeds attained by the TGV. Unlike traditional trains that shared tracks with freight and slower passenger services, the TGV operated on specially constructed lines. These tracks were designed to accommodate higher speeds, characterized by gentle curves and slight gradients. Consequently, the TGV could achieve and maintain velocities exceeding 300 km/h (186 mph) without compromising on safety or comfort. The advanced engineering behind these tracks marked a significant leap forward in rail infrastructure, setting new benchmarks for speed and efficiency.

Economically, the TGV has had a profound impact on tourism and regional connectivity across France and beyond. Cities that once seemed distant from each other became easily accessible, fostering greater economic interaction and cultural exchange. For instance, regions like Provence and Brittany experienced surges in tourist activity, invigorating local economies and creating numerous job opportunities. Businesses benefited from quicker and more efficient logistics, allowing for faster movement of goods and personnel between key commercial hubs. This improved connectivity bridged economic gaps and supported equitable regional development, uplifting both urban and rural areas.

In addition to speed and economic benefits, the TGV has excelled in providing a superior passenger experience, combining comfort, punctuality, and onboard amenities to attract travelers. Seats are ergonomically designed to offer maximum comfort even on long journeys, with ample legroom and reclining options. Passengers enjoy clean and well-maintained interiors, reflective of the high standards set by the service. Punctuality remains a hallmark of TGV operations, with extensive measures implemented to minimize delays and ensure timely arrivals.

Onboard amenities further enhance the travel experience, catering to diverse passenger needs. High-speed internet is available, enabling business travelers to work efficiently during their commute. Dining cars offer a variety of meals and beverages, ranging from casual snacks to elaborate full-course menus. Children's play areas and family-oriented services make the TGV an attractive choice for individuals traveling with young ones, ensuring a stress-free journey.

Germany's ICE

Germany's InterCity-Express (ICE) system stands as a testament to the country's ambition to modernize and enhance its rail services, becoming one of Europe's premier high-speed trains. Emerging in the 1980s from a desire to rejuvenate the national railway network, the development of ICE was driven by the need for speed, efficiency, and improved passenger experience.

The modernization effort began with comprehensive planning and investment. Germany sought to create a system that was not only technologically advanced but also user-friendly. The first ICE trains, officially inaugurated in 1991, were designed to operate at speeds exceeding 250 kilometers per hour, ensuring rapid transit across major cities. This significant speed improvement over traditional rail services allowed passengers to traverse long distances quickly, making rail travel an attractive alternative to air and road transport.

One of the core features of the ICE is its direct, no-transfer routes, which significantly reduce travel time and enhance usability. For instance, routes such as Berlin to Munich can be traveled without changing trains, offering convenience and time savings. This operational model minimizes the hassle usually associated with train travel, where passengers often have to switch trains multiple times. By providing direct connections between key cities, the ICE maximizes efficiency and appeals to both business travelers and tourists. The reliability and punctuality of these direct routes further bolster the system's reputation, making it a preferred choice for many.

Partnerships with other rail systems have been instrumental in expanding the reach of the ICE network. Collaborations with France's TGV and the Netherlands' trains exemplify how cross-border cooperation can enhance service offerings. These partnerships allow seamless travel experiences for passengers who can now enjoy uninterrupted journeys across different countries. For example, an ICE train traveling from Frankfurt might connect seamlessly with a TGV to Paris, providing a swift and convenient option for international travelers. This interconnectedness not only broadens the network but also fosters greater economic and social integration within Europe.

Marketing strategies highlighting the environmental benefits of high-speed rail have been crucial in attracting eco-conscious travelers. The ICE system promotes itself as a green alternative to air and car travel, emphasizing its lower carbon footprint and energy efficiency. Campaigns focus on the substantial reductions in CO_2 emissions that high-speed trains offer compared to airplanes or automobiles. This messaging resonates particularly well with today's environmentally aware consumers who prioritize sustainable travel options. Moreover, the German government supports this narrative by investing in renewable energy sources to power the trains, further solidifying the ICE's image as an environmentally friendly mode of transport.

The design and comfort of the ICE trains also play a vital role in their popularity. Spacious seating, onboard amenities such as Wi-Fi, dining facilities, and quiet zones cater to diverse passenger needs, enhancing the overall travel experience. The ergonomic design of seats ensures comfort during long journeys, while panoramic windows provide scenic views of the countryside, adding an aesthetic pleasure to the trip. These features collectively create a pleasant and efficient travel environment, encouraging repeat usage among passengers.

Safety has always been a priority in the development of the ICE system. Advanced engineering and rigorous maintenance protocols ensure the high reliability and safety standards of the trains. Equipped with cutting-edge braking systems and real-time monitoring technologies, the trains are designed to handle varying operational conditions effectively. Regular safety drills and continuous staff training further contribute to maintaining a flawless safety record, instilling confidence among travelers.

The economic impact of the ICE system extends beyond passenger convenience. The development of high-speed rail corridors has stimulated regional economic growth by improving accessibility and connectivity. Cities connected by ICE lines benefit from increased tourism and business activities, contributing to local economies. Additionally, the construction and expansion of the ICE network have created numerous jobs, from railway operations to hospitality services supporting the influx of travelers.

Looking at future prospects, the ICE system continues to innovate with plans for faster trains and expanded routes. Research into alternative fuels and zero-emission technologies is underway, aiming to make the trains even more sustainable. Continuous improvements in infrastructure, such as upgraded tracks and modernized stations, promise to enhance the efficiency and capacity of the network further. These ambitions reflect Germany's commitment to maintaining the ICE as a cornerstone of European high-speed rail.

Spain's AVE

Spain's pursuit of modernizing its transport system took a significant leap in the 1990s with the initiation of the AVE (Alta Velocidad Española) project. The goal was clear: to provide an efficient, high-speed rail network that could compete with other forms of transportation, particularly air travel. Spain's strategic investment in this infrastructure aimed at revolutionizing domestic travel, reducing journey times between major cities, and promoting regional development.

From its inception, the AVE network has been a catalyst for economic growth and social transformation within Spain. It allowed for rapid movement across the country, encouraging increased domestic tourism. By making distant cities more accessible, the high-speed trains fostered greater interaction and exchange between regions. This, in turn, supported local economies as tourists flocked to explore new areas, boosting hospitality, retail, and other related sectors. Moreover, the improved connectivity facilitated business travel, enabling professionals to attend meetings and conferences without the hassle of long road trips or airport delays.

The design of the AVE itself played a crucial role in its success. These trains were not just fast; they were engineered with cutting-edge aerodynamics to maximize safety and efficiency. The streamlined shape of the trains minimized air resistance, allowing them to achieve higher speeds while maintaining stability and safety. Advanced braking systems and sophisticated signal systems also contributed to ensuring that the trains could operate at such high velocities without compromising passenger security. This meticulous attention to design and technology helped build public confidence in high-speed rail as a reliable and safe mode of transport.

Sustainability has always been a priority for the AVE project. Recognizing the environmental impact of transportation, Spanish authorities implemented several initiatives to measure and improve the energy efficiency of these high-speed trains. One such initiative was the adoption of regenerative braking systems, which convert kinetic energy into electrical power that can be reused or stored. This not only reduces energy consumption but also cuts down on greenhouse gas emissions. The use of lighter materials in train construction further enhances energy efficiency by reducing the overall weight of the trains, thereby lowering the amount of energy required to reach and maintain high speeds.

Another noteworthy aspect of AVE's sustainability efforts is its alignment with Spain's broader carbon footprint goals. By offering a greener alternative to air and road travel, the AVE network contributes to the reduction of harmful emissions. High-speed trains typically emit significantly less CO_2 per passenger kilometer compared to airplanes and cars. Therefore, promoting rail travel over other, more polluting forms of transport aligns well with national objectives to combat climate change. Additionally, the expansion of the AVE network encourages the development of cleaner energy sources, such as wind and solar power, to support its operations.

The positive outcomes of the AVE project extend beyond just environmental benefits. Socially, it has had a profound impact on fostering inclusivity and bridging regional disparities. By connecting less economically developed areas with major urban centers, the AVE has opened up new opportunities for education, employment, and cultural exchange. Residents of smaller towns now have better access to jobs, universities, and healthcare facilities located in larger cities, enhancing their quality of life.

Furthermore, the AVE network stands as a testament to Spain's capability to execute large-scale infrastructure projects successfully. It showcases the potential of well-planned and efficiently managed public transport systems to transform a nation's economy and society. The project has set benchmarks in rail technology, design, and sustainable practices that other countries look to emulate. Its success story serves as an inspiration to policymakers, urban planners, and transportation enthusiasts worldwide who are keen on developing similar high-speed rail networks.

Cross-border interoperability

Cross-border interoperability among European rail networks represents a remarkable achievement in the realm of transportation. This interconnectedness simplifies international travel for passengers and stands as a testament to collaborative efforts across nations with diverse cultures and languages. As Europe continues to lead in high-speed rail innovation, examining the significance of this cooperation is crucial.

The interconnectedness of national networks plays a significant role in transforming the way people travel across Europe. One of the most notable benefits is the ease with which passengers can traverse multiple countries without complicated transfer processes. For instance, someone traveling from Paris to Berlin can now enjoy a seamless journey, thanks to the integration of various national systems. This network synchronization saves time and reduces the hassle associated with changing trains multiple times, thus making rail travel a more appealing option compared to air or road transport.

Collaborative infrastructure projects have significantly contributed to these improvements by linking major cities across France, Germany, and Spain. These projects include the Eurostar connecting London to Paris and Brussels, and Thalys connecting Paris with Amsterdam through Belgium. Such collaborations require substantial investment and political will but ultimately result in a highly efficient and cohesive rail system. By pooling resources and expertise, these countries can create a network that not only boosts their individual economies but also strengthens regional ties.

Examining these European models can inspire similar infrastructure investments in the U.S. and Canada. Currently, North American high-speed rail projects lag behind those in Europe, primarily due to fragmented planning and funding issues. However, taking lessons from Europe's success could guide policymakers in creating a more integrated and efficient rail system. The development of cross-border rail networks in Europe demonstrates that overcoming such challenges is possible through strategic planning and collaboration. By studying these models, North America could identify best practices and potential pitfalls, leading to more successful high-speed rail initiatives.

Addressing language and cultural differences is another critical aspect of fostering positive experiences for passengers. In a continent as diverse as Europe, communication barriers can pose significant challenges. However, by implementing multilingual signage, announcements, and customer service, European rail networks ensure that travelers from different linguistic backgrounds can navigate the system with ease. These measures contribute to a more inclusive and user-friendly environment, encouraging more people to choose rail travel.

Moreover, cultural differences also need consideration. For example, catering to local preferences in terms of food and amenities can enhance the travel experience. Offering region-specific services and products on board trains can make passengers feel more at home, even when they are far from their native country. This attention to detail not only improves customer satisfaction but also builds loyalty, encouraging repeat travel.

Furthermore, the significance of cross-border interoperability extends beyond convenience and customer satisfaction. It plays a vital role in promoting sustainability and reducing carbon emissions. High-speed trains are known for their energy efficiency compared to cars and airplanes. By creating a robust and interconnected rail network, Europe contributes to global efforts in combating climate change. The reduction in air travel, as more people opt for trains, leads to a significant decrease in greenhouse gas emissions, aligning with the EU's environmental goals.

Additionally, the economic benefits of an integrated rail network cannot be overlooked. Efficient rail connections stimulate tourism, boost local economies, and create job opportunities. Cities connected by high-speed rail often see increased business travel, conferences, and tourism, leading to higher revenue and economic growth. For instance, the introduction of high-speed rail between Madrid and Barcelona has significantly boosted tourism and commerce in both cities.

Importantly, the European model of cross-border interoperability sets a precedent for global cooperation in infrastructure development. It shows that nations with different political systems, economic conditions, and cultural backgrounds can work together towards a common goal. This cooperation serves as a blueprint for other regions aiming to develop or improve their rail networks.

Funding models and government support

Exploring the success of high-speed rail networks in Europe, it becomes clear that funding structures and government initiatives play crucial roles. With budget constraints always presenting a challenge, European nations have resorted to diverse funding avenues to support the development and maintenance of high-speed rail systems.

One of the most effective strategies employed is the use of public-private partnerships (PPPs). These collaborative arrangements allow governments to leverage private sector investment and expertise, thereby reducing the financial burden on public coffers while still ensuring the completion of large-scale infrastructure projects. An example of this can be seen in Italy, where the high-speed rail operator Italo was developed through a PPP model, drawing investments from various private entities. This method not only helps in securing the necessary funds but also brings efficiency and innovation to the project.

In addition to public-private partnerships, the European Union has been instrumental in facilitating funding for transport projects across its member states. The EU provides grants and subsidies aimed at enhancing connectivity and supporting sustainable transport systems. Various programs, such as the

Connecting Europe Facility (CEF) and the European Regional Development Fund (ERDF), offer significant financial support to help countries develop and improve their high-speed rail networks. For instance, Spain's AVE network expansion received substantial funding through these EU mechanisms, enabling it to extend high-speed rail services to more regions and enhance overall travel efficiency.

Moreover, the level of investment in high-speed rail often correlates with the cultural and political valuation of rail travel within a nation. In countries where rail travel holds significant value and is culturally embedded, investment levels tend to be higher. France, for example, has long been a proponent of rail travel, which is reflected in substantial governmental support for its TGV network. The French government has consistently prioritized rail infrastructure, recognizing its benefits for both economic growth and environmental sustainability.

Another critical aspect of optimizing funding for high-speed rail involves integrating relatable elements such as car-sharing and station redevelopment into the broader transportation strategy. Car-sharing initiatives, when linked with high-speed rail stations, provide seamless last-mile connectivity, enhancing the convenience and attractiveness of rail travel. This integrated approach not only improves passenger experience but also opens up new revenue streams and potential funding sources. Germany's Deutsche Bahn, for example, has successfully incorporated car-sharing services at its ICE train stations, thereby increasing patronage and maximizing the utility of its high-speed rail network.

Station redevelopment projects also play a pivotal role in optimizing funding. Revamping old or underutilized train stations into modern, multifunctional hubs can attract private investment and generate additional revenue through commercial activities. The redevelopment of London's King's Cross Station is an exemplary case. This project transformed the station into a vibrant urban space with retail outlets, offices, and recreational areas, attracting more passengers and generating considerable revenue, which can be reinvested into the rail network.

While public funding and government initiatives provide the backbone for high-speed rail projects, innovative approaches and strategic integrations enhance their feasibility and success. The collaboration between public and private sectors, coupled with EU support, ensures that high-speed rail remains a viable and flourishing mode of transport across Europe.

Peter Wretzky

Final Insights

This chapter explored the development and success of high-speed rail networks in Europe, focusing on key examples such as France's TGV, Germany's ICE, and Spain's AVE. By examining these case studies, we have seen how dedicated tracks, advanced engineering, and strategic investments have significantly boosted speed, efficiency, and passenger satisfaction. Each system has demonstrated the economic benefits of improved connectivity, including increased tourism, business opportunities, and regional development. Furthermore, the environmental advantages of high-speed rail, such as lower carbon emissions and energy efficiency, highlight its importance as a sustainable transportation solution.

The collaborative efforts that enable cross-border interoperability among European rail networks further enhance the appeal of high-speed rail travel. By simplifying international journeys and integrating various national systems, Europe has created a cohesive and efficient network. Funding models, including public-private partnerships and EU support, play a critical role in sustaining and expanding these systems. As policymakers, urban planners, and transportation enthusiasts reflect on these findings, they can draw valuable lessons to inspire similar successes in other regions, ultimately contributing to more effective and sustainable public transport solutions globally.

Chapter Nine

Environmental Benefits of Rail Travel

R ail travel offers substantial environmental benefits, making it a pivotal element in sustainable transportation solutions. Its potential to significantly reduce greenhouse gas emissions sets it apart from other modes of transport like automobiles and airplanes. As the world grapples with climate change, rail systems present an energy-efficient alternative that minimizes overall carbon footprints, making them an attractive option for both policymakers and the public.

In this chapter, we will delve into the diverse ways rail travel mitigates environmental impact. We will explore the lower carbon emissions associated with trains, particularly when compared to cars and planes, highlighting studies that show their effectiveness. Additionally, we will examine the comprehensive life cycle analysis of rail systems, including construction, maintenance, and operation phases. The role of federal and state regulations in promoting cleaner rail technologies will also be discussed, alongside the importance of public awareness and education in driving demand for rail-based travel. Case studies from various countries will provide real-world examples of successful rail system implementations, offering valuable insights for future policy development.

Reducing Carbon Emissions

Rail travel is increasingly recognized for its potential to significantly reduce greenhouse gas emissions, offering an important environmental benefit. Compared to automobiles and planes, rail systems are far more energy-efficient and environmentally friendly. By understanding and promoting these advantages, we can make a compelling case for greater policy support and public investment in rail infrastructure.

One of the most striking benefits of rail travel is its lower carbon footprint. Studies have shown that trains emit substantially less CO_2 per passenger mile than both cars and airplanes. For example, a typical car emits approximately 4.6 metric tons of carbon dioxide annually based on an average fuel efficiency of about 25 miles per gallon. In contrast, trains, especially electric ones, can move a vast number of passengers with only a fraction of these emissions. High-speed rail, in particular, stands out as an effective alternative to short-haul flights, which are notorious for their high levels of emissions relative to distance traveled.

However, it's not just the operational phase where rail outshines other modes of transport. A comprehensive life cycle analysis illustrates that rail systems have consistently lower emissions throughout their entire life span—from construction to maintenance and operation. Building a rail network does require significant initial energy and material input, but this cost is generally lower than that of constructing highways or airports. Rail tracks, once laid, can last for decades with minimal upkeep compared to constantly resurfacing roads or maintaining flight infrastructure. Furthermore, the energy used to power trains, particularly those running on electricity from renewable sources, is far cleaner than the fossil fuels consumed by cars and planes.

Federal and state regulations play a crucial role in incentivizing greener rail technologies. Policy frameworks can be designed to encourage the development and adoption of less polluting trains, such as those powered by electricity generated from renewable sources or hybrid models that combine traditional engines with battery technology. Governments can offer tax incentives, grants, and subsidies to companies investing in research and development of eco-friendly rail technology. Additionally, implementing stringent emission standards for both new and existing trains can drive operators to upgrade their fleets, phasing out older, less efficient models in favor of greener alternatives.

Public awareness and education are equally essential in shifting travel behavior towards rail options. While policies and technologies provide necessary structural support, public perception ultimately drives demand. Educating the populace on the environmental benefits of choosing rail over road or air travel can foster significant changes in transportation habits. Campaigns that highlight the carbon savings and overall reduction in pollution associated with rail travel can resonate with environmentally conscious individuals and groups. Moreover, raising awareness about the convenience, safety, and affordability of modern rail systems can help dismantle any lingering misconceptions and build a strong public affinity for train travel.

Several case studies underline the success of concerted efforts to promote rail travel. In Europe, countries like France, Germany, and Spain have invested heavily in high-speed rail networks, which dramatically cut travel times and emissions between major cities. In Japan, the Shinkansen, or bullet train, has become a model of efficiency and sustainability, demonstrating how advanced rail systems can transform national transportation landscapes. These examples serve as powerful testaments to the potential benefits awaiting countries willing to prioritize rail infrastructure.

To translate these lessons into actionable change, governments must develop clear and impactful policies that champion rail travel's environmental advantages. Federal and state authorities need to collaborate on creating cohesive frameworks that align with broader climate action goals. This might include integrating rail development plans within national and regional transportation strategies, ensuring seamless connections between different transit modes to maximize accessibility and convenience.

Additionally, fostering public-private partnerships can accelerate the deployment of green rail technologies. By working with private sector stakeholders, governments can leverage innovation and investment to build modern, efficient rail systems. These collaborations can also facilitate knowledge exchange and the scaling of best practices across borders, enhancing the global push towards sustainable transportation solutions.

Rail travel's potential to mitigate environmental harm is immense, making it a key player in our fight against climate change. Encouragingly, the mechanisms to harness this potential—be it through technological advancements, regulatory measures, or public engagement—are well within our reach. By focusing our efforts on reducing emissions, incentivizing cleaner technologies, and educating the public, we can create a robust foundation for a greener, more sustainable future.

Energy Efficiency Comparisons

Rail travel stands as a beacon of energy efficiency when compared to personal vehicles and air travel. To understand this, we must first delve into the concept of energy consumption per passenger mile, a crucial metric for gauging transportation impact on the environment. Trains excel in this area, using considerably less energy per passenger mile than cars or airplanes. This is primarily because trains can carry a significantly greater number of passengers at once, spreading out the energy cost over many individuals.

Trains achieve this superior energy efficiency through their ability to operate on dedicated tracks with minimal stops and starts. Unlike cars, which often face the inefficiencies of traffic congestion and frequent idling, trains maintain a consistent speed over long distances. This continuity reduces the amount of energy wasted and contributes to a lower overall energy consumption. Airplanes, although efficient at high speeds, spend considerable amounts of fuel during takeoff and landing cycles, impairing their overall efficiency compared to rail.

Another promising aspect of rail travel's environmental advantages is the integration of renewable energy sources into rail systems. The potential for using solar and wind power in this sector is particularly encouraging. Several rail systems around the world have already begun incorporating such renewable sources. For instance, some European countries are experimenting with solar panels installed along railway lines or atop train carriages. These installations can harness significant amounts of solar energy, reducing dependence on traditional fossil fuels.

Wind energy also offers tremendous potential for rail systems. Railways can be strategically placed in areas with high wind potential, allowing for the installation of wind turbines near the rail lines. The electricity generated from these turbines can then be fed directly into the rail network, providing a steady supply of clean energy. Moreover, advancements in renewable energy storage solutions mean that excess energy generated during windy periods can be stored and used later, ensuring a reliable power supply even when wind conditions are not optimal.

The electrification of trains is another major step toward enhancing energy efficiency and sustainability. Diesel-powered trains, while more efficient than personal vehicles, still rely on fossil fuels and emit greenhouse gases. In contrast, electric trains can be powered by a variety of energy sources, including renewables. The shift from diesel to electric propulsion not only reduces emissions but also enhances operational efficiency. Electric trains accelerate faster, require less maintenance, and offer smoother rides, making them more attractive to passengers and operators alike.

Countries like Japan and France have long demonstrated the benefits of electrified rail networks. Their high-speed trains, known as Shinkansen and TGV respectively, operate almost exclusively on electricity, showcasing remarkable efficiency and minimal environmental impact. These systems have become benchmarks for other nations looking to reduce their transportation sectors' carbon footprints.

Technological advancements in locomotive design and onboard energy management systems further bolster the energy efficiency of modern rail travel. Today's trains are equipped with regenerative braking systems that convert kinetic energy back into electrical energy during braking. This reclaimed energy can then be reused, significantly reducing overall power consumption. Additionally, newer locomotives are often lighter and more aerodynamic, minimizing resistance and energy use.

Innovations do not stop at the trains themselves. Modern rail infrastructure is designed with energy efficiency in mind. For example, optimized scheduling and improved signaling systems ensure trains run on time, reducing energy wastage due to delays and unscheduled stops. Smart grid technology allows for better energy distribution and load balancing, ensuring that electricity is used where it's needed most without excess waste.

In addition to the technological aspects, policy and public investment play critical roles in promoting energy-efficient rail travel. Governments and urban planners need to prioritize rail systems in their transportation agendas. Investments in rail infrastructure, subsidization of electric and hybrid trains, and incentives for research into new technologies can drive the sector toward greater sustainability. Collaborative efforts among nations can also foster shared learning and development, propelling global advancements in rail technology.

Energy management extends beyond just the trains and infrastructure. Efficient land use and urban planning around railway stations can contribute to broader energy savings. Dense development around transit hubs encourages higher ridership, maximizing the energy efficiency of each train journey. Such planning promotes the use of public transport over private vehicles, further amplifying energy savings and reducing environmental impact.

All these factors combined make rail travel an exceptionally viable option for sustainable transportation. As we transition towards a greener future, embracing energy-efficient models like rail travel will be pivotal. By understanding the inherent advantages of rail systems—lower energy consumption per passenger mile, integration of renewable energy, electrification benefits, and technological innovations—we can appreciate the significant role rail travel plays in our environmental landscape. This knowledge can inform policy decisions, guide urban planning, and influence individual choices toward more sustainable travel options.

Urban Congestion Alleviation

Rail transport presents a compelling solution to urban congestion, bearing significant environmental benefits and societal advantages. The growing adoption of passenger rail can substantially decrease road traffic and vehicle miles traveled (VMT), mitigating the environmental footmarks of vehicular emissions. In busy metropolitan areas where traffic congestion is a chronic problem, increased rail usage offers a viable alternative by providing efficient and frequent service that encourages commuters to leave their cars at home.

Case studies from cities like New York and various European metropolises serve as testament to the transformative impact of effective rail systems. In

New York City, the extensive subway network moves millions of people seamlessly each day, reducing the number of individual cars on the road. Similarly, European cities such as Amsterdam, Berlin, and Paris have long embraced rail as a central component of their urban transportation strategy. These rail systems do not only ease the daily commute but also alleviate the strain on urban roads, leading to smoother traffic flows and reduced pollution levels.

The benefits of reduced congestion extend beyond environmental impacts, promoting social equity and accessibility. Efficient rail systems provide increased mobility options for citizens across different socioeconomic spectra. Individuals who may not own a car or prefer not to drive have access to affordable and reliable transportation. This democratization of mobility ensures everyone, including lower-income populations, the elderly, and those with disabilities, can navigate the city with ease. Thus, rail transport contributes to a more inclusive urban environment where transportation barriers are minimized.

Furthermore, integrating rail into urban planning aligns closely with long-term sustainability initiatives. Cities that prioritize rail infrastructure in their developmental plans set the groundwork for sustainable growth. Planning regulations can encourage high-density development around rail hubs, reducing urban sprawl and preserving green spaces. This strategic approach promotes compact, walkable communities centered around transit, which reduces the demand for new road construction and minimizes habitat disruption.

For policy makers and urban planners, embracing rail involves leveraging its long-term benefits through thoughtful integration into broader city frameworks. Aligning new rail projects with existing urban development plans can amplify their positive effects. For instance, incorporating rail stations into mixed-use neighborhoods encourages residents to rely on public transit instead of personal vehicles, thereby contributing to lower carbon footprints. By fostering pedestrian-friendly environments around these stations, cities can stimulate local economies and enhance community well-being.

The role of rail in achieving social equity cannot be overlooked. Accessible transportation helps bridge gaps in opportunities, allowing individuals to participate more fully in economic, educational, and recreational activities. A well-planned rail system not only caters to current transportation needs but also anticipates future demographic shifts and growth patterns. Establishing equitable transit-oriented developments ensures that benefits are dispersed widely across urban populations.

Urban planners should consider the potential of rail systems to act as catalysts for revitalizing underdeveloped areas. Investing in rail infrastructure often leads to economic rejuvenation, creating jobs during construction and operation while attracting businesses to newly accessible locations. This symbiotic relationship between rail and urban prosperity underscores the multifaceted value of rail investments.

Guidelines for integrating rail into urban planning entail prioritizing connectivity, affordability, and inclusivity. Rail projects should be designed to interconnect with other modes of transport, such as buses, bikes, and pedestrian pathways, forming a cohesive and comprehensive network. Ensuring that rail systems remain affordable guarantees wide usage and supports low-income travelers. Moreover, inclusivity mandates that stations are equipped with facilities catering to all individuals, regardless of physical capability.

Long-term sustainability goals are furthered by rail's lesser reliance on fossil fuels compared to traditional road traffic. As cities increasingly adopt electric and renewable-powered trains, the environmental footprint of urban travel decreases. Policymakers need guidelines that support the transition to cleaner energy sources for rail systems, complementing broader climate action plans.

Land Use and Conservation

Developing passenger rail systems can significantly influence land use by promoting denser urban development and conservation areas. This shift in land use is crucial for creating sustainable and livable cities. One of the primary ways rail travel supports better land use is through smart growth principles. Smart growth emphasizes developing around transit hubs, which encourages more compact, walkable urban centers.

By concentrating development around railway stations, cities can reduce the need for sprawling suburbs and long commutes. This leads to a more efficient use of land and resources, as people live closer to their workplaces and amenities. It also reduces dependence on automobiles, decreasing traffic congestion and pollution. For example, cities like Tokyo and New York have successfully implemented rail-centric development, resulting in bustling urban centers with high accessibility and reduced environmental impact.

Rail lines also serve as preservation corridors for green spaces and landscapes. By designating certain areas along rail routes as protected zones, cities can maintain natural habitats and scenic beauty. This not only conserves biodiversity but also offers residents recreational spaces, improving overall quality of life. The presence of rail lines can discourage haphazard development, ensuring that open spaces remain undeveloped and protected. Examples of this can be seen in European cities like Zurich, where rail networks run parallel to green belts, providing both efficient transport and beautiful natural vistas.

Policy changes and zoning adjustments are vital for facilitating rail-centered urban development. Governments can implement policies that prioritize investment in rail infrastructure and support transit-oriented development (TOD). Zoning laws can be reformed to allow higher density construction near rail stations, making it easier for developers to create mixed-use buildings that combine residential, commercial, and recreational spaces. For instance, Portland, Oregon, has utilized TOD strategies to enhance its urban fabric, integrating rail transit with housing and business developments seamlessly.

Community engagement plays a critical role in harnessing local input for land use decisions. Involving residents in the planning process ensures that development meets the needs and desires of the community. Public forums, surveys, and workshops can provide valuable feedback on proposed projects, leading to more targeted and effective use of available land. Engaging with the community also fosters a sense of ownership and pride in local rail projects, increasing public support and utilization.

Implementing smart growth principles requires a clear understanding of local contexts and needs.

Guidelines for smart growth emphasize developing dense, mixed-use neighborhoods around transit hubs. These areas should be pedestrian-friendly, with amenities such as shops, schools, and parks within walking distance. Promoting alternative modes of transportation, like biking and walking, further reduces reliance on cars. Creating a network of connected, vibrant communities around rail stations can transform urban landscapes, making cities more sustainable and enjoyable to live in.

Preservation of green spaces along rail lines is another essential aspect of sustainable development. Guidelines for preserving these areas include establishing buffer zones to protect ecosystems and wildlife. Additionally, rail projects can incorporate green infrastructure, such as rain gardens and green roofs, to manage stormwater and improve air quality. In Amsterdam, for example, the city's extensive network of canals and green spaces integrates seamlessly with its rail system, demonstrating how urban areas can balance development and conservation effectively.

Zoning changes and policy adjustments are necessary to support rail-centered growth. Guidelines for these changes involve revising building codes to allow higher densities near rail stations and encouraging mixed-use development. Incentives such as tax breaks or grants can motivate developers to invest in rail-adjacent properties. Implementing performance-based zoning, which focuses on outcomes like sustainability and efficiency, can help achieve desired goals. Cities like Minneapolis have adopted flexible zoning practices to encourage the integration of rail transit into urban development plans.

Community engagement is essential for successful rail-focused land use. Guidelines for engaging the community include transparent communication about project goals and benefits and soliciting input from diverse stakeholders. Participatory planning processes can build trust and ensure that projects align with community values and priorities. Involving local businesses, neighborhood associations, and advocacy groups in decision-making can lead to more inclusive and equitable development outcomes. Barcelona's approach to community-led urban planning serves as an excellent example, where residents have a significant say in how their neighborhoods evolve around rail networks.

Rail Transport in Climate Change Mitigation Policies

Rail transportation plays a significant role in national and international climate change mitigation strategies. Governments around the world recognize that reducing greenhouse gas emissions from the transportation sector is crucial for meeting their climate goals. Rail travel, with its lower carbon footprint compared to road and air transport, emerges as a critical component in these plans. Countries are increasingly incorporating rail into their climate policies because of its potential to significantly cut emissions.

For instance, many governments have set ambitious targets to increase rail usage among commuters and freight transport. This shift not only reduces traffic congestion but also curbs the emissions associated with conventional vehicles. As more trains run on electricity—potentially drawn from renewable sources —these benefits will only grow. National strategies often involve investing in high-speed rail networks and improving existing infrastructure to make rail travel more appealing. Furthermore, policy incentives such as subsidized tickets or tax benefits aim to encourage more people to choose trains over cars or planes.

International collaborations and consortia also play a pivotal role in promoting rail expansion for climate goals. For example, the European Union has been a strong proponent of cross-border rail initiatives, supporting projects that link various countries through extensive rail networks. These collaborations make it easier for passengers and freight to move seamlessly across borders, thereby reducing the reliance on environmentally harmful modes of transport. Another illustrative example is the

International Union of Railways (UIC), which fosters global cooperation in creating sustainable rail systems. By sharing best practices and technological advancements, these international bodies help accelerate the adoption of greener rail solutions worldwide.

Guidelines developed within these consortia are essential for standardizing rail operations and ensuring environmental benefits. They could include recommendations on energy-efficient train designs, eco-friendly construction practices, and optimized scheduling to reduce idle times. Such guidelines ensure that rail projects, regardless of where they are implemented, adhere to high environmental standards.

Tracking the emissions from rail travel under global frameworks necessitates transparent metrics. Accurate data collection and reporting mechanisms are vital for assessing rail's impact on emission reduction efforts. International agreements like the Paris Agreement expect signatories to monitor and report their progress in lowering greenhouse gas emissions, and rail travel must be part of this equation. Developing robust metrics involves understanding various factors, such as the type of energy used by trains, the efficiency of rail networks, and the extent of their utilization.

Establishing these metrics not only aids in compliance with international treaties but also boosts public trust. When people see clear evidence of rail's environmental advantages, they are more likely to support rail-related policies and investments. Transparency enables policymakers, researchers, and the general public to track advancements, identify areas needing improvement, and celebrate successes in reducing emissions. Guidelines for establishing these metrics might cover methodologies for calculating emissions per passenger kilometer, accounting for energy sources, and integrating new technologies into emission tracking systems.

Future policy recommendations can further integrate rail into broader climate initiatives and urban resilience plans. Urban planners and policymakers should consider how rail can complement other sustainable transport options like cycling, walking, and electric buses. Creating multimodal transportation hubs where people can easily switch between different forms of green transport maximizes the environmental benefits.

Policies could also focus on developing transit-oriented developments (TODs) around rail stations. These are mixed-use residential and commercial areas designed to maximize access to public transport, which can reduce dependency on private cars and promote higher density living. TODs can lead to more efficient land use, conserving open spaces and minimizing sprawl. Additionally, integrating rail into disaster resilience plans ensures cities can rely on robust, low-emission transportation even during emergencies, thereby enhancing overall urban resilience against climate impacts.

Policy guidelines in this area might suggest approaches for integrating rail with bus lines, bike-share programs, pedestrian pathways, and even carpool services. They could also include best practices for community engagement to ensure that new developments meet local needs and preferences while advancing sustainability goals. Encouraging active participation from citizens can enhance the success of rail-centered urban planning initiatives.

Final Insights

This chapter has thoroughly examined the environmental benefits of adopting passenger rail as a sustainable mode of transportation. By highlighting the significant reduction in carbon emissions, energy efficiency, and the integration of renewable energy sources, it becomes evident that rail travel presents a viable solution for reducing our environmental footprint. The case studies from various countries further illustrate how effective rail systems can transform national transportation landscapes and contribute to broader climate action goals.

In addition to environmental advantages, the adoption of passenger rail can alleviate urban congestion, promote social equity, and support sustainable land use. Efficient rail systems offer affordable, reliable transportation options for all citizens, fostering more inclusive urban environments. Integrating rail into urban planning not only reduces traffic congestion but also encourages higher-density development around transit hubs, preserving green spaces and reducing urban sprawl. Overall, embracing passenger rail as a key element of our transportation strategy can pave the way for a greener, more sustainable future.

Chapter Ten

Economic Impacts of Revitalizing Passenger Rail

R evitalizing passenger rail in America offers a plethora of economic benefits that can dramatically transform communities and regions. Investing in passenger rail infrastructure is not just about improving transportation options; it acts as a catalyst for job creation, local economic growth, and long-term economic sustainability. The potential for stimulating various sectors of the economy through such investments makes this an important area of focus for policymakers, urban planners, and those passionate about sustainable development.

In this chapter, we will explore the direct and indirect job creation opportunities generated by passenger rail projects, highlighting the significant boost to employment sectors ranging from engineering to hospitality. We'll also delve into how improved rail services can stimulate local economies along rail corridors, enhancing connectivity and supporting small businesses. Additionally, we'll examine the long-term economic sustainability provided by consistent investments in rail technology and infrastructure improvements. Through detailed analysis and real-world examples, this chapter will demonstrate how revitalizing passenger rail can lead to vibrant, economically robust communities across America.

Job Creation and Economic Stimulus

Economic Impacts of Revitalizing Passenger Rail

Investing in passenger rail infrastructure can significantly influence economic landscapes, primarily through job creation. In this section, we'll delve into how these investments generate employment directly and indirectly, leading to broad economic benefits.

Direct Employment Opportunities

One of the most immediate impacts of investing in rail infrastructure is the creation of jobs for engineers, construction workers, and skilled tradespeople. These projects require extensive planning, design, and engineering expertise. Engineers are crucial in drafting efficient routes, designing safe and reliable rail systems, and solving environmental and logistical challenges. For example, the construction of high-speed rail lines necessitates advanced engineering solutions to ensure safety and efficiency.

Construction workers form the backbone of any rail project. From laying tracks to building stations, their labor is instrumental in bringing rail infrastructure to life. Skilled tradespeople such as electricians, welders, and technicians are also essential, handling the complex installations and ensuring that the systems operate smoothly. Projects like the Los Angeles Metro expansion or the California High-Speed Rail have seen thousands of jobs created for local communities.

Indirect Job Creation

Beyond direct employment, new rail services support ancillary industries such as tourism, hospitality, and retail. A well-connected rail network increases accessibility to various destinations, encouraging more people to travel. This influx benefits businesses that rely on foot traffic. Hotels, restaurants, and shops near train stations experience a boost in visitors, translating to increased sales and the need for additional staff.

For example, imagine a small town gaining a new railway connection. Local businesses would likely see an uptick in customers, encouraging new establishments to open. This ripple effect can rejuvenate entire areas, fostering economic vitality and growth. Tourism, a sector that thrives on ease of access, particularly benefits from improved rail services. Iconic tourist cities like New York, Chicago, and San Francisco become even more attractive when easily reachable by train, drawing more visitors and, subsequently, more spending.

Sustained Employment and Wealth Generation

The employment generated by rail investments extends beyond construction phases. Operative positions in rail companies, including conductors, ticket clerks, maintenance crews, and administrative roles, offer long-term stable employment. The ongoing necessity of maintaining and operating rail systems ensures that these jobs remain relevant.

Sustained employment bolsters wealth generation and economic stability within communities. Regular income allows families to invest in property, education, and other goods, stimulating local economies. When individuals have disposable income, they spend it on diversified services like healthcare, entertainment, and personal development, further multiplying economic benefits.

Peter Wretzky

Technological Advancements in Rail Systems

As rail systems evolve, technological advancements create specialized job opportunities in tech-related rail services. Modern railways increasingly incorporate smart technology, requiring software developers, data analysts, and cybersecurity experts. Innovations such as automated train controls, real-time tracking systems, and predictive maintenance software need continual updates and supervision. This field opens up high-paying tech jobs, contributing to economic growth and attracting a younger, tech-savvy workforce.

Technological hubs like Silicon Valley could see collaborations with rail companies to pioneer cutting-edge transport solutions. Sustainable technologies aimed at reducing carbon footprints also present opportunities. Developing energy-efficient trains or integrating renewable energy sources into rail operations requires innovation and skill, broadening the spectrum of available jobs.

Boosting Local Economies Along Rail Corridors

Enhanced passenger rail services play a critical role in revitalizing local economies, particularly those situated along rail corridors. The impact of these improvements can be seen in several key areas: enhanced connectivity, thriving small businesses, infrastructure enhancements, and bolstered regional tourism. Each of these factors contributes to the economic health and sustainability of the communities they serve.

Firstly, enhanced rail connectivity facilitates easier access to urban centers and other regions. This increased accessibility not only promotes the movement of people but also goods, services, and information. When rail lines are improved or newly introduced, they provide residents with more efficient travel options, reducing the reliance on automobiles and decreasing traffic congestion. This connectivity makes commuting more feasible, allowing people to live in more affordable suburban or rural areas while working in urban centers. It also opens opportunities for businesses to tap into larger markets, increasing their customer base and potential revenue streams. As travel becomes more convenient and reliable, it can spur residential growth and encourage investment in local real estate, further boosting the economy.

Small businesses stand to gain significantly from increased foot traffic brought by rail passengers. Stations often become hubs of activity, drawing both daily commuters and occasional travelers. These visitors create demand for various services such as dining, retail shopping, and personal care, providing a steady flow of customers for nearby businesses. For example, coffee shops, restaurants, and convenience stores located near rail stations often report higher sales volumes due to the constant influx of passengers looking for quick meals or snacks before boarding their trains. Additionally, the establishment of new rail lines can spark the creation of business districts around stations, transforming underutilized areas into vibrant commercial zones. This phenomenon can lead to increased employment opportunities and the overall financial health of the community.

Rail projects typically lead to broader infrastructure enhancements that go beyond the railway itself. These projects often require improvements to surrounding roadways, pedestrian paths, and public spaces to support the increased movement of people. In some cases, entire neighborhoods undergo revitalization efforts, including facelifts for old buildings, upgrades to utilities, and the development of green spaces. Such comprehensive enhancements not only improve the aesthetic appeal of the area but also increase property values and attract further investments. For instance, the introduction of high-speed rail in certain regions has led to the modernization of stations, which then become catalysts for broader urban renewal projects, benefiting the entire community.

Moreover, rail services have the potential to significantly bolster regional tourism by connecting key attractions. Tourist destinations that were previously hard to reach by car or airplane become more accessible through efficient rail networks. This ease of access encourages domestic and international tourists to explore multiple locations within a region, thereby spreading economic benefits across a wider area. Tourists traveling by rail tend to spend more time at their destinations, contributing to local economies through spending on accommodation, dining, and entertainment. Rail-tourism initiatives, such as scenic routes or heritage trails, can highlight cultural and historical assets, attracting niche markets and enhancing the overall tourist experience.

Investment in Technology and Innovation plays a crucial role in these rail revitalization projects. These advancements not only enhance the efficiency and safety of rail operations but also stimulate economic growth by creating tech-related job opportunities and fostering innovation ecosystems. Modern rail systems often incorporate cutting-edge technologies like automated ticketing, real-time tracking, and advanced signaling. These innovations streamline operations and improve user experiences, making rail travel more appealing and competitive. By investing in such technologies, regions can position themselves as forward-thinking and attractive to both residents and businesses. The ripple effect of this technological progress can be felt across various sectors, boosting productivity and economic resilience.

Peter Wretzky

Increase in Tourism and Mobility

In the realm of modern transportation, few methods hold as much potential for shaping economic landscapes and promoting sustainable practices as the revitalization of passenger rail systems. At its core, this subpoint examines how an enhanced passenger rail system fosters increased mobility and tourism, contributing to local economies and broader economic structures.

First and foremost, a robust passenger rail network can significantly impact tourism by incorporating underserved areas into tourist itineraries. Small towns and rural regions that were previously overlooked due to accessibility issues now become viable destinations. For example, a scenic area known only to locals could attract nature enthusiasts and vacationers willing to take a leisurely train ride. This influx of tourists brings new revenue streams to these communities, supporting local businesses such as hotels, restaurants, and shops. The ripple effect extends to job creation within these service sectors, ultimately boosting the local economy.

Furthermore, the appeal of sustainable rail travel cannot be overstated, especially among environmentally conscious travelers. As global awareness of environmental impacts grows, many tourists seek out eco-friendly options for their trips.

Rail travel offers a lower carbon footprint compared to other forms of transportation like cars and airplanes. By choosing trains, tourists not only reduce their ecological impact but also contribute to the demand for more sustainable travel options. In return, this increased demand encourages further investments in green technologies and practices within the rail industry, creating a positive feedback loop that benefits both the environment and the economy.

Rail services also play a pivotal role in encouraging urban exploration and multi-destination trips. Unlike car travel, which often involves long hours of driving and parking hassles, or air travel, characterized by security lines and limited city-to-city connections, trains offer a comfortable, hassle-free alternative. Passengers can move easily between cities, making it feasible to visit multiple destinations in one trip. For instance, a traveler can explore historical landmarks in one city, enjoy culinary delights in another, and wrap up with a visit to a cultural festival in a third— all within a single vacation. This fluidity not only enhances the travel experience but also ensures that spending is spread across various regions, fostering economic growth in multiple locations.

Improved rail connections also bolster local mobility, benefiting residents just as much as tourists. Enhanced connectivity allows people living in smaller towns or suburban areas to commute efficiently to urban centers for work, education, or leisure activities. This increased mobility can lead to demographic shifts, with individuals opting to live in more affordable, quieter areas while maintaining access to urban amenities. Over time, this shift can stimulate real estate markets in these smaller communities, raising property values and spurring local development projects. Additionally, easier access to larger cities can attract businesses seeking to expand their reach, thus creating job opportunities and further energizing local economies.

Moreover, the ways in which improved rail systems intersect with tourism are multifaceted. Special tourist trains or routes designed specifically with sightseeing in mind enhance the attractiveness of rail travel. Whether it's a wine country tour, a historical route, or a beachfront journey, themed train experiences draw niche market tourists who prioritize unique travel experiences. These specialized tourist packages not only boost ticket sales for rail operators but also encourage partnerships with local attractions and service providers, creating a symbiotic relationship that amplifies economic benefits.

Additionally, a well-maintained and efficient rail system promotes greater inclusivity in travel. Not all tourists have access to private vehicles or prefer the stress associated with driving. Rail travel offers an accessible and convenient option for families, elderly travelers, and individuals with disabilities. Stations equipped with necessary facilities and services ensure a more inclusive travel experience, tapping into a wider segment of the population and increasing overall ridership. Higher ridership means greater revenue for rail networks and more funds available for continuous enhancements and expansions, reinforcing the cycle of improvement and economic gain.

Importantly, the integration of passenger rail systems with existing public transportation networks enhances the convenience and appeal of rail travel. Seamlessly connecting trains with buses, trams, and metro systems makes it easier for travelers to reach their final destinations without facing the challenges of last-mile connectivity. Effective integration ensures that both tourists and local residents can maximize the utility of the rail system, leading to higher usage rates and increased economic activity surrounding transit hubs. Businesses near these transportation nodes, such as cafes, retail stores, and entertainment venues, stand to benefit significantly from the consistent foot traffic generated by commuters and travelers alike.

In essence, an enhanced passenger rail system is more than just a mode of transport; it is a catalyst for economic revitalization, fostering increased mobility and tourism, thereby bringing widespread benefits to communities. By opening up previously inaccessible regions to travelers, appealing to environmentally conscious tourists, facilitating urban exploration, and improving local mobility, passenger rail systems create thriving ecosystems where economic sustainability and growth are achievable goals.

The broader implications of a revitalized rail network extend beyond immediate economic gains. Long-term investments in rail infrastructure set the stage for sustained economic benefits, aligning with global goals of sustainable development and equitable growth. For policymakers and urban planners, championing passenger rail systems represents a forward-thinking approach to addressing transportation challenges, revitalizing local economies, and promoting a future where mobility and economic prosperity go hand in hand.

Cost-Benefit Analysis of Rail Investment

An in-depth examination of the economic implications of rail investments versus the costs associated with these projects reveals a complex but ultimately compelling narrative. Developing passenger rail infrastructure involves significant financial outlays. Initial expenditures include land acquisition, engineering design, construction of tracks and stations, rolling stock procurement, and integration with existing transportation networks.

These costs can escalate due to unforeseen challenges such as geological issues, regulatory compliance, and community objections.

Despite high upfront costs, the potential for substantial financial returns makes rail investment appealing. Passenger rail systems often generate revenue through ticket sales, advertising spaces, and leasing retail areas within stations. Moreover, rail services typically experience higher ridership compared to other forms of public transport, leading to consistent income streams. Long-term revenue generation becomes more feasible as more people choose rail for their daily commute or travel, reducing the reliance on initial funding.

Financial returns extend beyond direct income from rail operations. The ripple effects on local economies are profound. Cities and towns connected by reliable rail services often see increased property values due to improved accessibility. Businesses benefit from easier transportation of goods and services, while residents enjoy enhanced mobility. This connectivity stimulates local economies by attracting new businesses, fostering job creation, and boosting spending in the vicinity of railway stations.

For instance, the Northeast Corridor in the United States demonstrates how strategic rail investments can yield significant economic benefits. This rail service connects major cities like Boston, New York, Philadelphia, and Washington D.C., supporting economic activity across multiple states. The corridor generates billions of dollars in economic output annually, highlighting a strong return on investment. Similarly, California's High-Speed Rail project, despite its escalating costs, promises to deliver long-term economic gains by enhancing regional connectivity, reducing traffic congestion, and lowering carbon emissions.

A comparative analysis of various rail projects across the country further elucidates this dynamic. Projects like Denver's Union Station redevelopment show that even localized rail improvements can rejuvenate entire neighborhoods. The station's transformation into a mixed-use transit hub spurred development around the area, creating a vibrant community space and significant economic uplift. Conversely, projects like the Honolulu Rail Transit have faced scrutiny due to cost overruns and delays. These examples underscore the importance of thorough planning, stakeholder engagement, and realistic budgeting in successful rail investments.

Moreover, financial assessments of rail projects can shift policy perspectives on transport funding. Traditional transportation policies have often prioritized highway expansions and air travel subsidies over rail investments. However, comprehensive economic evaluations illustrate the broader societal benefits of passenger rail, including reduced road congestion, lower greenhouse gas emissions, and enhanced overall quality of life. By presenting a clear picture of the long-term advantages, policymakers can make more informed decisions about allocating public funds.

One essential consideration is the role of public-private partnerships (PPPs) in mitigating financial risks. PPPs leverage private sector efficiency and innovation while sharing the financial burden between public and private entities. Successful PPPs, like the Brightline rail service in Florida, showcase how private investment in passenger rail can lead to profitable ventures. Brightline, now rebranded as Virgin Trains USA, serves densely populated urban centers, providing a faster and more efficient alternative to driving or flying within the state. This model not only reduces taxpayer burden but also attracts private capital into public infrastructure projects.

As we evaluate the costs and benefits of rail investments, it is vital to address the environmental and social dimensions as well. Rail systems are inherently more sustainable than road or air transport, consuming less energy per passenger mile and producing fewer emissions. By investing in rail, communities can move towards greener transportation solutions, fulfilling broader sustainability goals. Additionally, rail systems enhance social equity by providing affordable and accessible transportation options to underserved populations, promoting inclusive growth.

Long-Term Economic Sustainability

Passenger rail systems create ongoing revenue streams for regional and federal economies through various avenues. Ticket sales represent an immediate source of income, yet their impact reaches far beyond the price per ride. Regular maintenance, service upgrades, and expansions necessitate consistent investment from both public and private sectors. These investments stimulate local businesses that supply materials and services, supporting a bustling network of economic activity. Furthermore, by improving accessibility via passenger rail, municipalities can attract new residents and businesses, leading to increased property values and higher tax revenues.

Rail development aligns seamlessly with sustainable economic goals, providing an eco-friendly alternative to car and air travel. Trains produce significantly lower greenhouse gas emissions per passenger mile compared to automobiles and airplanes. This reduction in carbon footprint is vital as cities and countries strive to meet climate targets and transition toward more sustainable transportation systems.

Choosing rail over other forms of transport helps mitigate congestion on roads and at airports, reducing overall infrastructure strain and maintenance costs. Sustainable rail systems often incorporate energy-efficient technologies and renewable energy sources, further contributing to environmental goals while fostering innovation in green industries.

Promoting equitable development in both urban and rural settings is another notable advantage of revitalized rail systems. Urban areas benefit from reduced traffic congestion and improved air quality as more people opt for train travel. Enhanced connectivity within cities enables more straightforward access to jobs, education, and healthcare, leveling the playing field for all socioeconomic groups. For rural communities, passenger rail provides critical links to larger markets and services that might otherwise be inaccessible. This connection can play a transformative role in stimulating local economies, offering residents greater mobility without relying on personal vehicles.

Forward-thinking rail investment also aligns with evolving transportation trends. As the demand for greener and more efficient travel options grows, rail systems present a viable solution. Modern trains equipped with the latest technology can offer high-speed, reliable service, making them competitive with other modes of transport. Electric and hydrogen-powered trains exemplify cutting-edge advancements, showcasing a commitment to innovation while addressing environmental concerns. Moreover, as urbanization continues, rail networks can expand in ways that accommodate population growth and shifting demographics, ensuring long-term sustainability.

In addition to these tangible benefits, the psychological appeal of rail travel should not be underestimated. The convenience and comfort of modern trains can make rail a preferred choice for many travelers, particularly those commuting daily to work or school. Faster journey times compared to road travel and less hassle than flying—no security checks or boarding delays—add to the attractiveness of rail. The predictability of train schedules provides peace of mind, encouraging regular use and thus reinforcing the financial viability of the rail system.

Continuous investment in rail infrastructure fuels employment opportunities, both directly and indirectly. Construction projects require a broad spectrum of skills, from engineering and design to manual labor and project management. Once operational, rail systems need staff for ticketing, customer service, maintenance, and administration. Indirectly, thriving rail networks boost related industries such as tourism, hospitality, and retail, which benefit from greater foot traffic and enhanced accessibility.

Another crucial aspect to consider is how rail systems can act as catalysts for broader urban and regional development. Transit-oriented development (TOD) is a concept that integrates residential, commercial, and leisure spaces around transit hubs, maximizing land use and supporting vibrant communities. Efficient rail services can reduce urban sprawl by encouraging denser, more sustainable living patterns. This integration promotes walkability and cycling, reducing dependence on cars and fostering healthier lifestyles.

Furthermore, revitalizing passenger rail contributes to social and economic resilience. In times of crisis, such as natural disasters or fuel shortages, having a robust rail network ensures that transportation remains available. Railways can operate under conditions that might halt road traffic or flights, providing a dependable means of moving people and goods. This reliability can be critical for emergency response efforts and maintaining continuity in daily life during challenging periods.

Investing in rail systems today prepares us for the future by aligning with technological and societal shifts. Autonomous and electric vehicle advancements signal a broader trend towards cleaner, smarter transportation solutions. Passenger rail can integrate with these developments, adopting cutting-edge technologies to enhance efficiency and user experience. Smart ticketing, real-time tracking, and improved safety measures are just a few examples of innovations that can transform rail travel into an even more attractive option.

Meanwhile, the global focus on sustainability and reducing carbon footprints emphasizes the importance of expanding rail infrastructure. Governments and organizations worldwide are setting ambitious targets to combat climate change, and rail offers a practical, scalable method to contribute to these goals. By prioritizing rail, policymakers can demonstrate commitment to environmental stewardship while delivering tangible benefits to communities.

Final Thoughts

This chapter has examined the economic benefits of investing in and revitalizing America's passenger rail system. By highlighting areas such as job creation, local economic stimulation, and long-term sustainability, it is clear that a robust rail network can significantly impact regional and national economies. Direct employment opportunities arise from construction and operational needs, while indirect benefits ripple out to ancillary industries like tourism and retail. The revitalized rail infrastructure not only creates immediate jobs but also offers sustained employment, benefiting communities over time.

Enhanced rail connectivity boosts local economies along rail corridors by improving access to urban centers and fostering business growth around stations. It also supports regional tourism by making destinations more accessible, encouraging travelers to visit multiple locations. Technological advancements in modern rail systems create specialized jobs, further driving economic growth. Overall, the chapter underscores how investment in passenger rail contributes to economic resilience, environmental goals, and social equity, demonstrating that a strong rail network is a cornerstone for sustainable development.

Chapter Eleven

Technological Innovations and Future Trends

T echnological innovations in passenger rail travel offer a glimpse into a future where efficiency, speed, and customer experience are significantly enhanced. By exploring emerging technologies and future trends, we can understand how these advancements promise to reshape the landscape of rail transport in the United States.

This chapter delves into various innovative solutions and concepts that hold substantial potential. It covers maglev technology, showcasing its ability to achieve unprecedented speeds through magnetic levitation. Automation and AI's role in streamlining train operations and maintenance is also examined, along with the futuristic prospects of Hyperloop systems. Furthermore, the chapter discusses advances in track and infrastructure materials, which are critical for enhancing safety and longevity. Finally, it highlights digital ticketing and other customer-centric improvements, emphasizing their impact on the overall travel experience.

Maglev Technology

Magnetic levitation (maglev) technology has the potential to revolutionize passenger rail travel, offering speeds and efficiencies previously unattainable with traditional rail systems. Unlike conventional trains that rely on wheels and tracks, maglev trains utilize powerful magnetic forces to lift and propel them forward. This reduction in physical contact means that friction is significantly minimized, allowing these trains to achieve much higher speeds. Typically, a maglev train can reach velocities over 300 miles per hour, showcasing a dramatic leap in rapid transit capabilities.

Countries like Japan and China have been pioneers in adopting maglev technology. Japan's Maglev Shinkansen and China's Shanghai Maglev are prominent examples of successful implementation. In Japan, extensive research and development efforts have resulted in a system that not only breaks speed records but also operates with remarkable efficiency and reliability. The Maglev Shinkansen, for instance, uses superconducting magnets cooled by liquid helium to create strong magnetic fields. These fields lift the train above the track and propel it forward with minimal energy loss. The Japanese experience emphasizes the importance of rigorous testing and phased deployment to ensure safety and performance standards are met.

China's Shanghai Maglev, which began operations in 2004, is another testament to the feasibility of this technology. Running between Longyang Road Station and Pudong International Airport, this maglev line covers a distance of approximately 19 miles in just over seven minutes. The Chinese project highlights the benefits of strategic route planning, targeting high-demand corridors where the investment in high-speed infrastructure can be quickly recouped through ticket sales and increased ridership. Additionally, lessons from both countries underscore the necessity of addressing technical challenges such as power consumption, electromagnetic interference, and system durability.

Despite the promising advantages, introducing maglev technology in the United States faces several obstacles, primarily concerning the high initial infrastructure costs. Building maglev lines requires substantial investments in specialized tracks, advanced propulsion systems, and sophisticated control mechanisms. Compared to conventional rail, these costs are exponentially higher, presenting a significant barrier to entry. For the U.S., which already struggles with funding for traditional rail maintenance and upgrades, allocating resources for maglev projects would require a seismic shift in budget priorities and public policy.

Furthermore, the political will to support such transformative projects must be galvanized at both the federal and local levels. Policymakers must recognize the long-term benefits of maglev adoption, including reduced travel times, lowered emissions due to electrification, and decreased congestion on highways and airspace. A coordinated effort involving legislative action to secure funding, streamlined regulatory processes, and public awareness campaigns to build support is essential. Moreover, drawing inspiration from global counterparts who have navigated similar challenges can provide valuable insights into effective strategies for overcoming bureaucratic hurdles.

Collaborating with the private sector could also play a crucial role in making maglev technology a reality in the U.S. Public-private partnerships (PPPs) can leverage the strengths of both sectors, combining governmental oversight and funding with private sector innovation and efficiency. Companies specializing in high-tech engineering, transportation logistics, and infrastructure development can bring in expertise and additional capital, reducing the financial burden on public coffers. These partnerships can also foster competitive bidding processes, ensuring that cost-effective solutions without compromising quality or safety are explored and implemented.

For maglev technology to gain traction in the U.S., a visionary approach to infrastructure planning is required. This includes identifying key routes where maglev can offer the most significant impact, such as densely populated urban corridors or regions with heavy commuter traffic. Feasibility studies and pilot projects can serve as proof-of-concept initiatives, demonstrating the viability and benefits of maglev to stakeholders and the general public. For instance, a pilot maglev route connecting major metropolitan areas on the East Coast or linking tech hubs in California could generate substantial interest and pave the way for broader acceptance and investment.

Guidelines for future prospects of maglev in America should include establishing a clear roadmap for development. First, initiate comprehensive feasibility studies to identify potential routes and assess environmental impacts. Second, develop a funding strategy that combines federal grants, state contributions, and private investments. Third, engage in public consultations to garner community support and address concerns. Fourth, adopt a phased implementation plan that begins with a pilot project, followed by gradual expansion based on performance outcomes and demand. Lastly, ensure ongoing research and adaptation to integrate technological advancements and emerging best practices globally.

Automation and AI in Rail Operations

Automation and artificial intelligence (AI) hold incredible promise for revolutionizing the efficiency and safety of passenger rail systems. Let's delve into how these technologies can streamline operations, adapt to real-time data, provide successful case studies from around the world, and address important ethical considerations.

Automation in passenger rail involves using technology to carry out routine tasks without human intervention. Scheduling and maintenance are two critical areas that greatly benefit from this. Automated scheduling systems can efficiently manage train timetables, ensuring optimal spacing between trains and reducing congestion on busy routes. These systems analyze vast amounts of historical data to predict peak travel times and adjust schedules accordingly, minimizing delays and maximizing track usage. Maintenance, another fundamental aspect of rail operations, also sees significant improvements through automation. Predictive maintenance technologies use sensors and AI-driven analytics to monitor the health of trains and infrastructure continuously. This proactive approach identifies potential issues before they become serious problems, thereby increasing safety and reducing downtime.

Intelligent systems take things a step further by adapting to real-time data. For instance, advanced AI algorithms can optimize train routes based on current conditions such as weather, passenger load, and unexpected incidents. If there is a sudden delay on one line, these systems can automatically reroute trains to maintain smooth service. This dynamic adaptation not only enhances operational efficiency but also provides passengers with a more reliable travel experience. Additionally, these intelligent systems contribute to energy efficiency. By constantly analyzing data on train speeds, braking patterns, and power consumption, they can recommend adjustments that reduce energy use and lower operational costs.

Several real-world examples illustrate the successful integration of automation in passenger rail systems. The London Underground, one of the world's oldest and busiest metro systems, has been a pioneer in adopting automated technologies. Its Victoria Line, largely operated by automated systems, showcases how such advancements can improve punctuality and reduce human error. The Docklands Light Railway, also in London, operates with minimal human intervention, offering a glimpse into a fully automated future. Sweden, too, provides compelling examples. The country's X2000 high-speed trains employ sophisticated automation for speed control and braking, resulting in smoother and safer journeys.

While the benefits of automation and AI in rail systems are evident, it is crucial to consider their ethical implications. One significant concern is job displacement. As machines take over tasks traditionally performed by humans, there is a risk of reduced employment opportunities in the rail industry. It is essential to strike a balance between technological advancement and maintaining jobs. Policymakers and industry leaders must collaborate to ensure that workers are retrained and redeployed in new roles created by these innovations.

Another ethical dimension involves the balance between human oversight and automation. While automated systems can handle most routine tasks, human operators are still vital for monitoring and decision-making in complex or emergency situations. Ensuring that there is always a human element in the loop can prevent over-reliance on machines and safeguard against potential system failures.

The discussion wouldn't be complete without touching on how these technologies can be responsibly implemented. Firstly, transparency in the deployment of automation and AI is paramount. Operators and passengers should be informed about how these systems work and what data they use. Secondly, continuous monitoring and regular updates of AI algorithms are necessary to address any biases or errors that might arise.

Hyperloop Concepts

The Hyperloop concept represents a bold, futuristic alternative to traditional passenger rail travel. By utilizing advanced technology, it proposes to revolutionize how people commute over medium to long distances. The core idea behind the Hyperloop is simple yet groundbreaking: passenger pods travel through low-pressure tubes at speeds that could exceed 600 miles per hour. This method of transit aims to reduce travel times drastically, making rapid transit a reality. Imagine a trip from Los Angeles to San Francisco in just about 30 minutes instead of hours by conventional trains or cars.

Pilot projects spearheaded by companies such as Virgin Hyperloop are leading the charge in bringing this vision to fruition. These initiatives aim to validate both the feasibility and technical progress of the Hyperloop system. For instance, Virgin Hyperloop has conducted successful tests showcasing the potential of their technology. During these trials, passenger pods achieved impressive speeds within controlled environments, paving the way for future real-world applications. Such pilot projects serve as crucial benchmarks, providing valuable data and insights needed to address any technical challenges and demonstrate the viability of Hyperloop systems to investors and policymakers.

However, despite the promising technology, the path to widespread implementation is fraught with significant hurdles. One of the most formidable barriers is the high capital investment required. Building the necessary infrastructure involves substantial upfront costs, including the construction of specialized low-pressure tubes and stations. Additionally, acquiring the requisite land poses another considerable challenge. In densely populated areas, securing large tracts of land for the installation of Hyperloop infrastructure can be both time-consuming and expensive. Moreover, existing land use regulations and community opposition can further complicate the land acquisition process.

Another aspect to consider is how the Hyperloop might integrate with existing transportation networks. Successful integration could create a multimodal transport system that would be highly appealing to riders. Imagine seamlessly transitioning from a local train or subway to a high-speed Hyperloop pod, reducing overall travel times and enhancing convenience. However, achieving such integration requires careful planning and collaboration between various transportation authorities and stakeholders. It's essential to ensure that the new system complements rather than competes with existing modes of transit. This collaboration could lead to an interconnected network where each mode of transport enhances the other's strengths, creating an efficient and user-friendly system.

The long-term implications for American rail are particularly intriguing. If integrated effectively, the Hyperloop could set a precedent for combining cutting-edge technology with traditional rail systems. This fusion has the potential to transform the landscape of passenger rail travel in the United States, promoting sustainability and offering faster, more convenient transit options. Adopting the Hyperloop could also stimulate economic growth by creating new jobs in engineering, construction, and operations while fostering innovations in related industries. However, it is vital to approach this transformation thoughtfully, considering both the opportunities and challenges it presents.

Advances in Track and Infrastructure Materials

In the realm of passenger rail travel, the materials used for tracks and infrastructure play a critical role in ensuring safety, durability, and efficiency. This section delves into the advancements in this area, highlighting innovations that promise to revolutionize the way we build and maintain rail systems.

First, it's essential to discuss the introduction of new composite materials and advanced designs. Traditional steel tracks, while robust, come with their own set of challenges, including susceptibility to wear and tear and significant maintenance requirements. Innovations in composite materials have led to the development of tracks that are not only more resilient but also boast an extended lifespan. These materials, often incorporating polymers and reinforced fibers, display superior resistance to environmental stressors such as temperature fluctuations and moisture. For instance, carbon fiber composites have become increasingly popular due to their strength-to-weight ratio, which enhances track performance while reducing the load on supporting structures.

The economic implications of these advancements are profound. By extending the lifespan of tracks, railway companies can significantly reduce both the frequency and cost of maintenance. Lower maintenance costs translate directly into operational savings, which can be reinvested in other areas such as service improvements or fare reductions. Furthermore, fewer track replacements mean reduced downtime, leading to more reliable and efficient rail services. The use of durable composite materials essentially ensures that tracks are less prone to failures, thereby enhancing overall safety for passengers and cargo alike.

Smart materials are another groundbreaking innovation shaping the future of rail infrastructure. These materials, embedded with integrated sensors, offer real-time monitoring capabilities that were previously unattainable. By continuously collecting data on various parameters such as stress levels, temperature, and vibrations, smart materials enable predictive maintenance strategies. This means that potential issues can be identified and addressed before they evolve into significant problems, thereby avoiding costly repairs and service disruptions.

For example, an integrated sensor within the track material can detect micro-cracks or anomalies long before they manifest as visible defects. Maintenance crews can then be dispatched to perform targeted repairs, ensuring that the tracks remain in optimal condition. Additionally, this real-time monitoring allows for a more efficient allocation of resources, as maintenance efforts can be directed specifically where they are needed, rather than following a predetermined schedule. The result is a more proactive approach to track management that maximizes both safety and efficiency.

Germany serves as a shining example of how advanced track materials can enhance rail system resilience. In regions where extreme weather conditions—including freezing winters and scorching summers—pose significant challenges, German railways have implemented advanced track materials designed to withstand such extremes. These materials exhibit excellent thermal stability, meaning they maintain their structural integrity across a wide range of temperatures. This is particularly important in preventing track buckling or cracking, issues that can compromise both safety and service reliability.

The success of Germany's approach underscores the importance of investing in high-quality materials that can adapt to varying environmental conditions. Other countries can look to Germany's experience as a model for improving their own rail infrastructure, particularly in areas susceptible to harsh weather. By doing so, they can ensure that their rail networks are better equipped to handle the challenges posed by climate change and other environmental factors.

Another promising avenue of research focuses on sustainable and recycled materials. As the world grapples with the effects of climate change, there is a growing emphasis on reducing the ecological footprint of industrial activities, including rail transport. Researchers are exploring ways to incorporate recycled materials into track construction, aiming to strike a balance between durability and environmental sustainability. For example, using recycled plastic in conjunction with traditional materials can produce tracks that are both strong and eco-friendly.

Moreover, sustainability-focused materials often come with the added benefit of cost savings. By leveraging locally sourced recycled materials, railway companies can reduce expenses associated with raw material procurement and transportation. This approach not only supports environmental goals but also contributes to the economic viability of rail projects. The shift towards greener materials reflects a broader commitment to sustainable development within the rail industry, aligning with global efforts to mitigate environmental impact.

Looking to future directions in material science, the focus is on developing even more sophisticated materials that can further enhance the performance and sustainability of rail infrastructure. For instance, nanotechnology holds great promise in this regard. By manipulating materials at the molecular level, it is possible to create tracks with unprecedented strength, flexibility, and resistance to wear. Such advancements could herald a new era of rail travel, where infrastructure is not only more durable but also capable of self-repairing minor damages, thereby extending its lifespan.

To guide future developments in this field, it's crucial to establish clear guidelines for the integration of new materials into existing rail systems. These guidelines should address key considerations such as compatibility with current infrastructure, long-term performance metrics, and environmental impact assessments. By doing so, policymakers and industry stakeholders can ensure that the transition to advanced materials is both seamless and beneficial.

Digital Ticketing and Customer Experience Improvements

The advent of digital innovations has revolutionized many sectors, and passenger rail travel is no exception. As we seek to improve the customer experience in rail travel, several key technological advancements stand out. These developments not only simplify existing processes but also introduce new levels of convenience and efficiency that were previously unimaginable.

One of the most transformative innovations is e-ticketing. Gone are the days when passengers had to wait in long lines to purchase paper tickets. E-ticketing systems allow travelers to buy their tickets online, whether through a website or an app, making the process quick and easy. An e-ticket can be stored on a smartphone or another electronic device, which reduces the need for physical tickets and hence, minimizes waste. Furthermore, e-ticketing provides real-time updates regarding train schedules. If a train is running late or there is a change in the platform, passengers can receive immediate notifications, allowing them to adjust their plans accordingly. The convenience and efficiency brought by e-ticketing cannot be overstated, as it enhances the overall travel experience while simultaneously reducing operational costs for rail companies.

In addition to simplifying ticket purchasing, digital innovations have significantly improved onboard services. One notable example is the availability of Wi-Fi on trains. In today's interconnected world, passengers expect to stay connected, even while traveling. Providing Wi-Fi access transforms what could be a tedious journey into an enjoyable and productive experience. Passengers can work, browse the internet, or stream entertainment, thereby making the most of their time while traveling. This service is particularly beneficial for business travelers who can use travel time efficiently to complete work-related tasks. Consequently, the availability of Wi-Fi can be a deciding factor for many passengers when choosing their mode of transport.

Looking beyond our borders, European models offer valuable insights into further enhancing the rail travel experience. For instance, Europe has successfully implemented interoperable ticketing schemes, where one ticket allows seamless travel across multiple types of transportation systems, including trains, buses, and trams. This interoperability simplifies travel planning and eliminates the need for passengers to purchase separate tickets for each leg of their journey. Imagine a traveler arriving by plane at a major European airport. With one ticket, they can easily transfer to a train, bus, or tram that takes them to their final destination. This level of integration greatly enhances convenience and efficiency, serving as a model that could be replicated in the United States to foster a more user-friendly transportation network.

With an eye toward the future, several emerging technologies promise to take these advancements even further. Biometric boarding is one such innovation poised to enhance security and streamline the boarding process. By utilizing facial recognition or fingerprint scanning, passengers can board trains quickly and securely, without the need for traditional tickets or identification documents. This not only speeds up the boarding process but also reduces the potential for human error and fraudulent activities. For example, a commuter simply walks through a biometric scanner, which verifies their identity and grants access to the train, all within a few seconds. This technology, already being tested in airports, could bring substantial benefits to the rail industry.

Another promising development is the use of blockchain technology for ticketing. Blockchain provides a highly secure and transparent method for issuing and verifying tickets, making it difficult for fraudsters to create counterfeit tickets. Additionally, blockchain can facilitate the transfer of tickets between individuals in a secure and verifiable manner. For instance, if a passenger is unable to travel and wishes to transfer their ticket to someone else, blockchain technology ensures that the transaction is legitimate and the new holder receives a valid ticket. Moreover, blockchain's decentralized nature means there is no single point of failure, further bolstering system security and reliability.

These innovations collectively highlight the transformative impact of digital technologies on the customer experience in rail travel. They provide practical solutions to common issues faced by passengers, such as the complexity of purchasing tickets, lack of connectivity, and cumbersome boarding procedures. Additionally, they offer a glimpse into a future where rail travel can be a seamlessly integrated, highly efficient, and secure mode of transportation.

It is essential to recognize that the successful implementation of these technologies requires collaboration among various stakeholders, including government agencies, rail companies, and technology providers. Policymakers and urban planners must work together to develop and enforce regulations that facilitate the adoption of these innovations while ensuring they align with broader transportation goals. Investments in infrastructure and technology are necessary to support these advancements. For instance, upgrading rail networks to support high-speed internet access or implementing biometric scanners at stations involves considerable planning and resources. However, the long-term benefits of enhanced passenger experience and operational efficiency make these investments worthwhile.

Bringing It All Together

This chapter has explored a variety of emerging technologies and future trends that hold the potential to transform passenger rail travel in the United States. With advancements like magnetic levitation (maglev) trains, automation, AI, Hyperloop concepts, and innovative track materials, the chapter highlights how these developments can significantly enhance efficiency, speed, and customer experience. Examples from countries such as Japan, China, the UK, and Sweden illustrate successful implementations of these technologies, offering valuable insights into their potential benefits and challenges.

Nonetheless, realizing these advances in the U.S. requires addressing several obstacles, including high infrastructure costs and political commitment. Strategies like public-private partnerships, phased implementation, and comprehensive feasibility studies are essential to overcoming these barriers. Furthermore, the integration of digital innovations, such as e-ticketing and onboard Wi-Fi, exemplifies the ongoing improvements in customer experience.

Peter Wretzky

By adopting a visionary approach and learning from global counterparts, the U.S. can pave the way for a modernized and efficient rail system that meets future transportation demands.

Chapter Twelve

Policy and Legislative Frameworks

P olicy and legislative frameworks play a crucial role in shaping the future of passenger rail in America. These frameworks serve as the foundation upon which rail systems are built, operated, and expanded, influencing everything from safety standards to funding mechanisms. Understanding the intricate relationships between federal and state responsibilities in rail policy provides essential insight for developing sustainable and efficient rail networks.

In this chapter, we will explore the historical context of how federal and state governments have shared and shifted responsibilities over time. We will examine current legislative frameworks and policies that impact passenger rail development, analyzing key federal initiatives like the Passenger Rail Investment and Improvement Act (PRIIA) and state-level innovations such as California's high-speed rail project. Additionally, we will delve into specific examples of how different states are implementing unique solutions tailored to their regional needs, highlighting the dynamic interplay between federal guidelines and local ingenuity in advancing America's passenger rail systems.

Federal vs State Responsibilities

The division of responsibilities between federal and state governments has a longstanding influence on the infrastructure and operational support for passenger rail systems in America. Understanding this division requires a glimpse into its historical context, an examination of current legislative frameworks, an analysis of federal policies, and examples of state-level innovations.

Historically, the management of passenger rail services in the United States has seen significant shifts in responsibilities between federal and state governments. Initially, during the early development of the rail industry in the 19th century, private companies primarily drove rail expansion with minimal government involvement. The federal government facilitated this growth through land grants and financial incentives to railroad companies, aiming to bolster westward expansion and economic development. However, as the industry matured and more complex operational challenges emerged, there was a gradual shift toward greater government oversight.

The rise of the 20th century saw increased federal intervention, particularly with the establishment of regulatory bodies like the Interstate Commerce Commission (ICC) to oversee rail rates and practices. States also began stepping in, enacting their own regulations to address regional needs and priorities. This dual-layered approach laid the groundwork for the modern division of responsibilities, which continues to evolve today.

Current legislative frameworks reflect this evolved relationship, characterized by a mix of federal oversight and state-level initiatives. At the federal level, the Department of Transportation (DOT) and the Federal Railroad Administration (FRA) play pivotal roles in setting safety standards, allocating funding, and ensuring compliance with national regulations. Key legislation, such as the Passenger Rail Investment and Improvement Act (PRIIA) of 2008, underscores the federal commitment to supporting and enhancing passenger rail services across the country.

On the state level, governments have enacted their own frameworks tailored to local circumstances and objectives. Some states, like California and New York, have even established dedicated rail authorities to manage regional rail networks and undertake ambitious projects like California's high-speed rail initiative. These state-driven efforts often involve collaboration with regional transit agencies and private sector partners to maximize efficiency and impact.

Federal policies, particularly major legislative acts, significantly impact passenger rail development. One notable example is the Fixing America's Surface Transportation (FAST) Act, enacted in 2015. The FAST Act provided critical funding and outlined strategic priorities for improving transportation infrastructure, including passenger rail. By allocating billions of dollars towards rail improvements and streamlining project approval processes, the FAST Act aimed to enhance the reliability and performance of the nation's passenger rail systems.

Federal initiatives like these also emphasize the importance of safety and innovation. Programs under the FRA focus on research and development to advance rail technology and improve operational safety. For instance, the Positive Train Control (PTC) system, mandated by federal law, leverages advanced technology to prevent train accidents caused by human error. Such federal mandates ensure consistent safety standards across state lines and foster technological advancement in the rail sector.

While federal policies set the stage, state-level innovations often lead the charge in implementing unique rail solutions that address specific regional needs. Take, for example, the Virginia Department of Rail and Public Transportation (DRPT), which has spearheaded initiatives to extend and improve passenger rail services within the state. Through strategic partnerships with freight rail companies and neighboring states, Virginia has successfully expanded its Amtrak routes and increased service frequency, providing more reliable and convenient options for passengers.

Another compelling example comes from Oregon, where the Oregon Department of Transportation (ODOT) has taken innovative steps to integrate passenger rail with broader multimodal transportation planning. ODOT's efforts include developing green corridors that promote sustainability and reduce environmental impact, showcasing how state-level initiatives can align with national goals while addressing local priorities.

Furthermore, states like Illinois and Washington have pioneered efforts to enhance passenger rail operations through targeted investments and policy adjustments. In Illinois, the state's involvement in the Chicago-to-St. Louis high-speed rail project exemplifies how state leadership can drive transformative infrastructure projects. Similarly, Washington State's commitment to improving its Cascades route illustrates a proactive approach to upgrading rail infrastructure and promoting cross-border travel with Canada.

These state-level initiatives highlight a critical aspect of the federal-state partnership: while federal policies provide overarching guidance and essential funding, state governments possess the flexibility and local knowledge necessary to adapt and innovate. This complementary dynamic allows for a diverse range of passenger rail solutions that cater to the unique characteristics and demands of each region.

Funding and Grants

Federal Funding Sources form the cornerstone of many passenger rail initiatives in America. The Federal Railroad Administration (FRA), under the Department of Transportation, is a primary source of capital and operational funds for these projects. The FRA administers various grant programs designed to enhance the nation's rail infrastructure, often focusing on safety improvements, modernizing aging equipment, and increasing service efficiency. A notable program is the Consolidated Rail Infrastructure and Safety Improvements (CRISI) grant, which provides funds for projects that improve rail safety, efficiency, and reliability. In addition to CRISI, the FRA also oversees the Federal-State Partnership for State of Good Repair Program, which assists states in maintaining and improving intercity passenger rail networks.

State and Local Funding Mechanisms play an equally significant role in shaping the financial landscape of passenger rail. State governments often allocate specific portions of their budgets for transportation infrastructure, including rail projects. For example, California has dedicated substantial resources through the California High-Speed Rail Authority, aiming to build a high-speed rail line that will connect major cities across the state. States may also leverage transportation bonds approved by voters to finance extensive rail renovations or new lines. At the local level, municipalities may implement tax initiatives like sales taxes or property taxes to generate revenue earmarked for public transportation projects. These localized funding efforts are crucial as they reflect the community's commitment and support, ensuring the longevity and relevance of rail services.

Grant Opportunities abound for entities seeking to undertake passenger rail initiatives, with a variety of options available from both public and private sectors. Public grants, such as those from federal or state agencies, are essential for securing substantial portions of project costs. Private grants, often offered by foundations and corporations with interests in transportation or environmental sustainability, also provide valuable funds. One illustrative example is the Transportation Investment Generating Economic Recovery (TIGER) grant, now known as BUILD (Better Utilizing Investments to Leverage Development). This competitive grant program supports projects that have a significant economic impact on a regional or national scale. Several cities have successfully utilized TIGER/BUILD grants to revitalize their rail systems, demonstrating the transformative potential of these funds.

Despite the availability of various funding sources, Challenges in Securing Funding remain a significant obstacle for many rail projects. Entities seeking financial support must navigate a complex landscape filled with stringent application processes, competing interests, and fluctuating political priorities. One major challenge is the competition for limited federal funds. With numerous applicants vying for the same pool of money, only projects with the most compelling cases receive funding. Additionally, matching fund requirements can present hurdles, as some grants necessitate that applicants provide a certain percentage of the total project cost from other sources. This condition can be particularly challenging for smaller municipalities or regions with limited financial resources.

Furthermore, the bureaucratic procedures involved in applying for and managing grants can be daunting. Detailed proposals, comprehensive financial audits, and strict compliance with reporting standards require expertise and resources that not all entities possess. This complexity often results in delays or even disqualification if errors are made. Political dynamics also play a critical role; shifts in government priorities at the federal or state level can lead to changes in funding availability or focus areas, impacting long-term planning and stability for rail projects.

The interplay between Federal Funding Sources, State and Local Funding Mechanisms, and Grant Opportunities illustrates the multifaceted nature of financing passenger rail initiatives. Federal programs administered by bodies like the FRA provide significant support, but state-specific allocations and local tax initiatives are equally vital, reflecting regional priorities and community support. The existence of diverse grant opportunities further enriches the financial landscape, offering avenues for innovation and development.

However, these funding mechanisms do not come without challenges. Entities seeking support must contend with rigorous application processes, competition for limited resources, and changing political landscapes. The complexities inherent in navigating these obstacles underscore the importance of strategic planning and collaboration among stakeholders. Clear communication, meticulous planning, and proactive engagement with funding bodies can enhance the chances of securing necessary funds.

Moreover, successful examples from states and municipalities highlight the potential of well-coordinated efforts in overcoming financial barriers. For instance, the collaborative approach taken by California's High-Speed Rail Authority and its strategic leveraging of federal, state, and local funds exemplify how integrated financing strategies can drive large-scale rail projects forward. Similarly, municipalities that engage their communities in supporting tax initiatives for public transportation demonstrate the power of local commitment in ensuring sustainable rail services.

Regulatory Hurdles

The regulatory landscape governing passenger rail in America is complex and multifaceted, with numerous agencies and regulations playing pivotal roles. This overview will delve into the existing regulatory bodies and their influence on rail operations.

The Federal Railroad Administration (FRA) is one of the primary entities responsible for overseeing railroad safety regulations. Established in 1966, the FRA sets and enforces safety standards to ensure that passenger and freight rail operations are secure. These standards cover a wide array of areas, including track quality, signal systems, and employee training. While the FRA's role is crucial for maintaining high safety standards, its stringent regulations can sometimes be seen as obstacles to rapid innovation and expansion within the sector.

Another key player in the regulatory framework is the Surface Transportation Board (STB), an independent federal agency charged with resolving railroad rate and service disputes and reviewing proposed railroad mergers. The STB's decisions can significantly impact the operational efficiency and financial health of passenger rail services. For instance, approval processes for new rail lines or expansions can be lengthy, delaying critical infrastructure projects.

Case studies provide concrete examples of how these regulatory frameworks have impacted rail initiatives. One notable case is California's High-Speed Rail project. Initiated with the promise of revolutionizing travel within the state, this project has encountered numerous regulatory hurdles. Environmental reviews mandated by both state and federal laws have caused significant delays. Moreover, compliance with FRA safety standards added layers of complexity and cost, illustrating how regulatory requirements can extend timelines and inflate budgets.

Conversely, there are instances where regulatory frameworks have facilitated progress. The Northeast Corridor (NEC), which runs from Boston to Washington, D.C., benefits from a more streamlined regulatory approach due to its historical significance and established infrastructure. The FRA, recognizing the strategic importance of the NEC, has provided grants and technical support that have aided in modernizing the corridor, demonstrating that flexible regulatory mechanisms can promote development.

The current regulatory environment also presents barriers to innovation. With advancements in technology, new opportunities for improving rail efficiency and safety emerge regularly. However, existing regulations can impede the adoption of these innovations. For example, outdated rules concerning train control systems may restrict the implementation of more advanced and potentially safer technologies. Similarly, stringent procurement rules can limit the ability of rail operators to quickly adopt newer, more efficient rolling stock.

Moreover, regulatory constraints often stifle operational advancements. For instance, the introduction of autonomous rail technology could significantly reduce operational costs and improve safety. Yet, current regulations do not adequately address the unique challenges and potentials of this technology, leading to uncertainty and hesitation among rail operators considering such investments.

Given these challenges, stakeholders need effective strategies for navigating the regulatory landscape. One essential approach is proactive engagement with regulatory bodies. Early and continuous communication can help align project goals with regulatory expectations, reducing the likelihood of unexpected obstacles. Establishing collaborative relationships with regulators can facilitate smoother project approvals and foster a more adaptive regulatory environment.

Another strategy involves leveraging public-private partnerships (PPPs). These collaborations can bring additional expertise and resources to rail projects, helping to meet regulatory requirements more efficiently. Additionally, private sector involvement can introduce innovative solutions that comply with existing regulations while enhancing project outcomes.

Stakeholders should also focus on comprehensive planning. Thorough environmental and safety assessments conducted early in the project lifecycle can identify potential regulatory challenges beforehand, allowing for timely adjustments and mitigations. This proactive planning helps avoid costly delays and ensures smoother project execution.

Training and capacity building are equally important. Investing in upskilling staff to better understand and navigate regulatory requirements can enhance a project's compliance profile. Knowledgeable staff can anticipate regulatory demands and develop plans that align with legal expectations, thereby reducing friction with oversight agencies.

Moreover, it is beneficial to advocate for regulatory reform. Engaging in policy dialogue with lawmakers and participating in industry associations can provide platforms to push for changes that foster innovation and reduce unnecessary regulatory burdens. By working collectively, stakeholders can influence the creation of more balanced regulations that support safety without hindering progress.

Finally, adopting a phased implementation approach can mitigate risks. Dividing large projects into smaller, manageable phases allows for incremental compliance checks and adjustments. This method not only makes regulatory approval processes more manageable but also provides opportunities to demonstrate compliance and success early on, building credibility with regulatory bodies.

Public-Private Partnerships (PPPs)

Public-private partnerships (PPPs) are collaborative agreements between government entities and private organizations aimed at achieving a common goal. In the realm of passenger rail systems, these partnerships can play a pivotal role in building efficient, cost-effective transportation networks. The essence of a PPP in the context of railroads is the combination of public oversight and private sector innovation and funding. This collaboration leverages the strengths of both parties, leading to better resource management, enhanced service delivery, and ultimately, improved passenger experiences.

The importance of PPPs cannot be overstated when discussing the modernization and expansion of passenger rail systems. Unlike traditional procurement methods that rely solely on public funding and management, PPPs introduce an element of competition and efficiency driven by private stakeholders. Governments may lack the capital required for extensive rail projects or the expertise needed for cutting-edge technological implementations. By engaging private firms with specific skill sets and financial power, projects can benefit from timely completion and innovative solutions. Additionally, PPPs often bring with them a degree of flexibility not usually found in entirely public endeavors, allowing for adaptive responses to changing circumstances and needs.

There are several successful models of PPPs that highlight their potential in transforming passenger rail systems. One notable example is the Denver Eagle P3 project, which stands as a benchmark for effective PPP implementation. This project involved designing, constructing, financing, operating, and maintaining three new commuter rail lines in the Denver metropolitan area. The public-private consortium successfully delivered the project ahead of schedule and within budget. The integration of private sector efficiency with public accountability ensured high-quality service standards while mitigating financial risks through shared responsibilities.

Another exemplary case is the UK's High Speed 1 (HS1) line, connecting London to the Channel Tunnel. The project was completed through a PPP model involving significant private investment. The success of HS1 is attributed to the meticulous planning that outlined clear roles and responsibilities for both public and private sectors. The project did not only deliver a state-of-the-art high-speed rail connection but also highlighted how PPPs can attract substantial private investments, thereby reducing the strain on public finances. These cases demonstrate that PPPs can lead to the successful realization of ambitious projects by effectively harnessing the capabilities and resources of both sectors.

Despite these successes, establishing PPPs in the rail sector is not devoid of challenges. One major obstacle lies in aligning the objectives of public and private partners. While governments aim to provide accessible and affordable services to the public, private companies often prioritize profitability. Balancing these aims requires detailed negotiation and a clear, legally binding framework that ensures mutual benefits without compromising public interests.

Moreover, regulatory hurdles can impede the formation of PPPs. Rail infrastructure projects demand compliance with numerous safety, environmental, and operational regulations. Navigating this complex regulatory landscape requires extensive expertise and can delay project timelines, escalating costs and deterring private investors. Another significant challenge is the allocation of risks. In PPP projects, risks such as construction delays, cost overruns, and revenue shortfalls need to be equitably distributed between public and private entities. Misaligned risk distribution can lead to disputes, project failures, and significant financial losses for both parties.

To address these challenges, it is essential to establish clear guidelines for crafting effective PPP agreements. Firstly, roles and responsibilities should be explicitly defined, ensuring that each party understands their commitments and stakes. Secondly, a robust legal framework must be established to oversee the partnership, providing mechanisms for dispute resolution and adjustments in response to unforeseen circumstances. Thirdly, transparent processes for risk assessment and distribution are crucial. Both parties need to agree on how risks will be managed and shared, ensuring that incentives align with the successful delivery of the project.

Looking toward the future, the landscape of PPPs in passenger rail is evolving, influenced by technological advancements and shifting societal needs. With the rise of smart cities and the increasing demand for sustainable transportation solutions, PPPs are likely to incorporate more innovative technologies and green practices. For instance, the advent of digital ticketing systems, real-time passenger information services, and the use of big data analytics offers new opportunities for enhancing rail services. Private companies specializing in technology can drive these innovations, making rail travel more efficient, user-friendly, and environmentally friendly.

Furthermore, as societies become more environmentally conscious, PPPs will need to focus on sustainability. This includes investing in cleaner energy sources, such as electrification of railways and the development of hydrogen-powered trains. These initiatives require substantial financial input and technical know-how, areas where private partners can play a critical role. By integrating sustainability goals into PPP agreements, passenger rail systems can reduce their carbon footprint and contribute towards broader environmental objectives.

Incentives for Rail Development

Governments have a pivotal role in fostering the development of passenger rail services through various incentives. These incentives not only encourage investment but also help align the interests of different stakeholders, including private investors, local communities, and policymakers. By strategically providing support, governments can drive growth in passenger rail infrastructure, creating a network that is both efficient and sustainable.

One of the primary tools for encouraging investment in rail infrastructure is tax incentives. Governments can offer tax credits or deductions to entities that invest in rail projects. For example, tax credits could be provided for capital investments in rail lines, stations, and related facilities. Such incentives reduce the overall cost of investment for private companies, making rail projects more financially attractive. Additionally, governments can implement deductions for expenses related to maintaining and upgrading rail infrastructure. These deductions can offset annual operational costs, ensuring that rail operators remain economically viable while delivering high-quality service.

Government grants and subsidies represent another crucial form of incentive aimed specifically at rail projects. Grants often come from federal, state, or local sources and are designated for various stages of development, such as planning, construction, and implementation. For instance, the Federal Railroad Administration (FRA) offers grants to improve the safety, efficiency, and reliability of passenger rail systems. These funds enable rail operators to undertake large-scale projects that might otherwise be financially infeasible. Subsidies, on the other hand, can help bridge the gap between operational costs and revenue, ensuring that passenger services remain affordable and accessible to the public. This financial support not only stimulates initial investment but also aids in the long-term sustainability of passenger rail services.

Regulatory and administrative support can significantly influence the initiation and success of rail projects. Streamlining the regulatory approval process is one way governments can provide this support. When regulatory barriers are minimized, the time and cost associated with starting new projects are reduced, making it easier for companies to move forward with their plans. Simplified regulations can also foster innovation by allowing operators to experiment with new technologies and operational models without being bogged down by outdated rules. Furthermore, governments can establish dedicated agencies or task forces to assist with navigating the complex web of regulations, thereby accelerating project timelines and reducing compliance costs.

Community and economic development incentives play a vital role in garnering local support and enhancing engagement for passenger rail projects. These incentives can take various forms, such as job creation programs linked to rail construction and operations, which directly benefit local economies. Governments can also promote transit-oriented development (TOD) around rail stations, encouraging mixed-use developments that combine residential, commercial, and recreational spaces. This approach not only boosts ridership by integrating rail services into daily life but also spurs local economic growth. Moreover, community grants aimed at improving infrastructure around rail stations—such as pedestrian pathways, bike lanes, and public amenities—can make rail travel more convenient and attractive to residents.

The strategic use of tax incentives can drive significant investment in rail infrastructure. Rail projects typically require substantial upfront capital, making them risky ventures for private investors. However, when governments offer tax credits for capital expenditures or deductions for operational expenses, these projects become much more appealing. For example, a company investing in new rail lines might receive a tax credit equivalent to a percentage of their total investment, effectively lowering their initial costs. Similarly, allowing deductions for maintenance and upgrades ensures that operators can keep their systems running smoothly without fearing financial strain. By reducing the financial burden on investors, tax incentives create a favorable climate for rail development.

Evaluating government grants and subsidies reveals their critical role in sustaining and expanding passenger rail services. Grants often target specific aspects of rail projects, such as safety upgrades, technological improvements, or network expansions. For instance, a grant from the FRA might fund the installation of advanced signaling systems designed to enhance operational safety and efficiency. These grants not only cover a portion of the project costs but also signal governmental commitment to rail infrastructure, attracting additional private investment. Subsidies ensure that even less profitable routes can continue operating, providing essential connectivity and supporting broader transportation networks. By offering financial assistance, grants and subsidies ensure that rail projects can progress from concept to reality.

Examining regulatory and administrative support highlights the importance of a conducive regulatory environment for rail project success. Stringent regulations can delay projects, increase costs, and deter investment. Conversely, streamlined regulatory processes can accelerate project timelines and reduce financial burdens. Governments can achieve this by revising outdated regulations, adopting flexible frameworks, and expediting approval processes. For instance, creating fast-track approval mechanisms for environmentally beneficial projects can encourage the adoption of green technologies in rail transport.

Additionally, establishing dedicated support teams within regulatory bodies can help stakeholders navigate regulatory requirements efficiently, minimizing administrative hurdles and fostering a proactive approach to compliance.

Community and economic development incentives are crucial for building local support and maximizing the benefits of passenger rail services. Job creation initiatives linked to rail projects can provide significant economic boosts to local communities. For example, constructing new rail lines and stations creates numerous employment opportunities in fields ranging from construction to ongoing operations and maintenance. Furthermore, governments can encourage TOD around rail hubs, promoting vibrant, walkable communities where people live, work, and play. This approach not only increases rail ridership but also stimulates local economies by attracting businesses and enhancing property values. Community grants for infrastructure improvements around rail stations can further enhance the appeal of rail travel, making it a preferred mode of transport for residents.

Summary and Reflections

The chapter highlighted the significant impact of policy and legislative frameworks on the future of passenger rail in America. It delved into the historical division of responsibilities between federal and state governments, illustrating how this relationship has shaped rail development over time. Key federal policies were discussed, including their role in setting safety standards, providing funding, and fostering technological advancements. The chapter also examined how states have harnessed their unique circumstances to drive innovative rail solutions that address local needs and collaborate effectively with federal initiatives.

Furthermore, the importance of various funding mechanisms, such as federal grants, state budgets, and local tax initiatives, was underscored. These financial sources are crucial for supporting rail projects amidst regulatory challenges, which can inhibit innovation and operational efficiency. By examining case studies and successful examples, the chapter demonstrated the complementary dynamic between federal oversight and state-level creativity. This synergy is essential for developing a diverse range of rail solutions tailored to regional demands, highlighting the critical role of policy and legislative frameworks in shaping America's passenger rail landscape.

Chapter Thirteen

Overcoming Societal Resistance

O vercoming societal resistance is crucial for fostering the adoption of passenger rail services. Public perception significantly impacts the success of such initiatives, and understanding how to shift these views can pave the way for greater acceptance and support. Explorations in this chapter delve into strategies that can positively influence public opinion on rail travel, presenting ways to bring about a collective change in mindset.

This chapter discusses multiple approaches to mitigate societal barriers to passenger rail adoption. It starts with emphasizing the advantages of rail travel, such as convenience, cost-effectiveness, and environmental benefits, which can make it more appealing to different demographics. Case studies from countries with successful rail systems are presented to provide tangible evidence of their benefits. Tailored communication strategies are also covered, showing how messages can be crafted to resonate with specific groups. Furthermore, community engagement methods that integrate rail discussions into local events and educational partnerships highlight how normalized conversations about rail can foster acceptance. Lastly, the importance of consistent and transparent communication from transportation authorities is underlined, demonstrating how keeping the public informed builds trust and support for rail initiatives.

Changing Public Perceptions

Altering public perceptions can play a pivotal role in fostering acceptance and support for passenger rail services. One effective way to do this is by highlighting the advantages of passenger rail. When people understand that rail travel offers convenience, cost-effectiveness, and environmental benefits, they are more likely to shift their focus away from any perceived inconveniences.

Convenience is a significant factor to emphasize. Passenger rail services often offer faster transit times compared to car travel, particularly in congested urban areas. They also provide a stress-free experience where passengers can relax, read, or work during their commute. Highlighting the punctuality and reliability of modern rail systems can further showcase the convenience offered by passenger rail.

Cost-effectiveness is another critical advantage. Rail travel can be more affordable than car travel when considering fuel costs, parking fees, and vehicle maintenance expenses. Additionally, public transportation can reduce the economic burden on families by providing an alternative to owning multiple vehicles. Emphasizing long-term savings and the cost benefits for frequent travelers can help change public attitude toward adopting passenger rail.

Environmental benefits cannot be overlooked. Rail travel is significantly more sustainable than car travel, reducing greenhouse gas emissions and decreasing the carbon footprint of commuters. By showcasing how passenger rail contributes to cleaner air quality and less traffic congestion, it becomes clear that supporting rail initiatives is an investment in a healthier future.

To foster acceptance, sharing examples of successful rail systems in other countries can be highly influential. Many countries, such as Japan, Germany, and Switzerland, have robust and efficient passenger rail networks. Highlighting the positive impact these systems have had on their respective societies can inspire confidence and optimism. For instance, Japan's Shinkansen, or bullet train, is renowned for its speed, safety, and reliability. Its success story can serve as a benchmark, demonstrating what is possible with proper investment and public support.

Germany's Deutsche Bahn and Switzerland's comprehensive train network are great examples of how integrated and customer-friendly rail systems can enhance mobility. These examples provide tangible evidence that well-planned and efficiently managed rail systems can thrive and benefit society. By presenting these case studies, the public can visualize the potential improvements passenger rail could bring to their daily lives.

Crafting messages tailored for specific demographics can increase the resonance and support for rail projects. Different groups have varied concerns and interests that must be addressed uniquely. For instance, younger generations might be more interested in the environmental benefits of rail travel, while older populations might prioritize comfort and reliability. Tailoring messages to highlight aspects most relevant to each demographic ensures that the communication is relatable and persuasive.

For students and young professionals, emphasizing affordability and the ability to use commuting time productively can be appealing. For families, focusing on safety, ease of travel, and financial savings can resonate more effectively. For seniors, ensuring that rail services are accessible, comfortable, and reliable would be key points to address. Creating diverse communication strategies that speak directly to these groups helps build widespread support by connecting with individuals on a personal level.

Increased presence of passenger rail in community conversations can normalize its existence and importance. Engaging communities through local meetings, forums, or even social media discussions allows residents to voice their opinions and concerns, fostering a sense of inclusion and ownership. This involvement can demystify rail travel and integrate it into the public consciousness as a viable and valuable mode of transportation.

Organizing community events around rail themes, such as "Rail Days" where citizens can experience rail travel firsthand, can also help normalize its presence. Rail enthusiasts and local representatives can engage with the public, answering questions and addressing misconceptions. By making rail travel a topic of everyday conversation, it becomes a familiar and accepted concept.

Additionally, strategic partnerships with local schools and universities can play an educational role. Collaborating with educational institutions to present the benefits and importance of passenger rail can instill a positive perception among younger generations. School programs that include field trips using rail services or curriculum modules on sustainable transportation can lay the groundwork for long-term acceptance and support.

Finally, consistent and transparent communication from transportation authorities about rail developments, progress, and benefits can keep the public informed and involved. Regular updates through various media channels, town hall meetings, and newsletters can maintain a steady flow of information, erasing doubts and building trust within the community.

Community Engagement and Participation

Active community involvement in rail projects can be a powerful tool to overcome societal resistance and foster acceptance. One of the primary methods to achieve this is by engaging local communities in the decision-making process. When community members are invited to participate, they feel valued and their unique perspectives are considered. This empowerment results in a more informed and supportive stakeholder group. For example, public meetings, workshops, and advisory boards can provide forums where residents express concerns and contribute ideas. These interactions not only democratize the planning process but also offer planners valuable insights into local needs and preferences.

In order to effectively engage these communities, it is crucial to connect rail discussions to local events. Local events, such as fairs, festivals, and town hall meetings, present excellent opportunities to raise awareness about rail projects. By integrating rail project discussions into these familiar and well-attended gatherings, planners can reach a broader audience and make the issue more relatable. For instance, setting up informational booths at a county fair or hosting a special session during a community festival can significantly increase visibility and relevance. This approach ensures that rail initiatives are part of the everyday conversations within the community, thereby normalizing the concept of rail travel.

Another vital strategy involves collaborating with respected community figures. Local leaders, whether they are elected officials, business owners, or activists, hold significant influence within their communities. Partnering with these individuals can lend credibility to rail projects and help sway public opinion. For example, gaining the support of a popular mayor or a revered community elder can have a ripple effect, encouraging others to view the project more favorably. Additionally, testimonials from local influencers can personalize the benefits of the rail initiative, making them more tangible for community members.

Establishing consistent communication channels is also essential in keeping the community informed and engaged. Regular updates through newsletters, social media, and community meetings can create a sense of transparency and trust. For example, a dedicated website or social media page can serve as a hub for all project-related information, updates, and feedback opportunities. This level of openness not only demystifies the project but also allows for continuous dialogue between planners and the public. Moreover, being responsive to community inquiries and concerns through these channels can further reinforce the collaborative nature of the project.

To illustrate these points, let's consider a hypothetical rail project in a mid-sized city. The city's transportation department decides to involve the community early in the planning stages by organizing a series of public workshops. These workshops allow residents to voice their opinions on proposed routes, station locations, and service features. The feedback collected is then used to refine the project, ensuring it aligns with the community's needs. During the summer, the department participates in the city's annual festival, setting up an interactive booth where attendees can learn about the rail project, ask questions, and provide input. This presence at a popular event helps to raise awareness and generate excitement about the initiative.

Simultaneously, the department partners with local leaders, including the city council members, business association presidents, and neighborhood association heads. These leaders become advocates for the project, sharing its benefits with their constituents and addressing any concerns. Their endorsement helps build credibility and trust among the community. Throughout the process, the department maintains an active online presence, regularly posting updates, answering questions, and collecting feedback through their website and social media pages. They also send out monthly newsletters to keep residents informed of the project's progress and upcoming events.

By following these guidelines, the transportation department successfully mitigates societal resistance and garners widespread local acceptance for the rail project. The community's involvement and contributions lead to a design that reflects their needs and desires, resulting in a more sustainable and supported initiative.

Addressing Concerns of Rural Areas

Addressing the concerns of rural communities is essential for gaining acceptance of passenger rail services. By recognizing and understanding their unique needs, we can ensure equitable rail development that benefits everyone, regardless of their geographical location. Rural populations often have different lifestyles and expectations from urban dwellers, which necessitates tailored solutions.

Understanding the distinct requirements of rural populations begins with acknowledging their daily realities. Unlike urban environments where public transport options are plentiful, rural areas might lack regular and efficient transportation systems. Thus, the introduction of passenger rail services must be seen as a significant improvement to their mobility. By conducting thorough research and engaging in direct dialogue with these communities, policymakers and planners can gather valuable insights into specific needs. For example, farmers may require transportation options that accommodate the timing of agricultural activities, while families might need access to schools, medical facilities, and markets. Identifying these distinct needs ensures that rail services are designed to fit seamlessly into rural life.

Designing inclusive rail services that accommodate rural lifestyles can greatly enhance acceptance. To do this, schedule flexibility is crucial. Rail services should operate at times that align with the routines of rural residents. For instance, early morning and late evening trains can cater to those whose workdays begin before dawn or end after sunset. Additionally, stations should be strategically located within reachable distances for most residents, reducing the need for long commutes to access rail services. This approach not only makes the service more convenient but also demonstrates a commitment to inclusivity and accessibility.

Furthermore, the development of passenger rail services can stimulate economic growth in rural areas, shifting perspectives and fostering acceptance. Improved connectivity brings numerous opportunities for economic activities. For example, local businesses can expand their reach to larger markets, and tourism can flourish with easier access to remote attractions. The presence of reliable transportation can attract new businesses and investors, spurring job creation and enhancing the local economy. Highlighting these tangible benefits through community engagement and public information campaigns is vital. When rural residents see the potential for economic upliftment, their support for rail projects can increase significantly.

Promoting how rail can lead to economic prosperity involves showcasing success stories from other regions. For instance, the revitalization of small towns in Europe through enhanced rail connectivity can serve as a powerful example. Local media coverage and community meetings can be utilized to present data and testimonials demonstrating the positive impacts of rail services on rural economies. This evidence-based approach can effectively counter skepticism and build confidence among rural populations.

Keeping rural communities informed about rail developments is another critical factor in fostering trust and acceptance. Transparency and consistent communication are key. Regular updates on project timelines, construction progress, and expected benefits help demystify the process and address any concerns promptly. Creating dedicated communication channels such as newsletters, community forums, and social media pages can facilitate this exchange of information. Engaging with local leaders and influencers who can advocate for the project further strengthens the relationship between rail developers and the community.

In addition to providing updates, involving rural communities in the planning process can enhance their sense of ownership and investment in the project. Public consultations, surveys, and feedback sessions can offer valuable insights and ensure that the final design reflects the needs and aspirations of the residents. This participatory approach can transform potential opposition into active support, as people feel heard and valued.

The importance of educating rural communities about the broader benefits of passenger rail cannot be overstated. Beyond immediate economic gains, rail transport offers environmental advantages by reducing reliance on personal vehicles and lowering carbon emissions. Raising awareness about these long-term benefits can foster a collective sense of responsibility towards sustainable transportation solutions. Environmental education programs, collaborations with schools, and partnerships with local environmental groups can amplify this message and create a culture of support for rail initiatives.

Moreover, addressing safety concerns is paramount. Educating rural communities about the safety measures implemented in rail projects can alleviate fears and build trust. Providing clear information on how the rail system enhances overall safety, such as reduced road traffic accidents and improved emergency response times, can reassure residents. Additionally, organizing safety drills and demonstrations can equip them with the knowledge and confidence to use rail services safely.

Accessibility is another concern that must be addressed to gain acceptance in rural areas. Ensuring that stations and trains are accessible to people with disabilities, the elderly, and young children is crucial. Implementing features like ramps, elevators, and designated seating areas shows a commitment to inclusivity. Furthermore, offering assistance programs for those who need help navigating the rail system can make it more user-friendly and welcoming.

Finally, affordability is a significant factor in rural acceptance of passenger rail services. Many rural residents may have limited financial resources, and expensive rail fares could deter them from using the service. Developing pricing strategies that consider the economic realities of rural populations, such as discounted rates for frequent travelers or subsidized tickets for low-income families, can make rail travel more appealing and accessible.

Marketing and Advocacy Strategies

Overcoming Societal Resistance

Promoting passenger rail initiatives in a manner that counters societal resistance requires strategic marketing and advocacy approaches. This subpoint will discuss distinct strategies to heighten the acceptance of passenger rail services by developing targeted marketing campaigns, utilizing emotional storytelling, collaborating with organizations supporting sustainable transport, and presenting clear information to challenge misconceptions.

Creating Targeted Campaigns

First, developing marketing campaigns that resonate with specific demographics is essential for fostering greater acceptance of passenger rail services. Different groups have unique needs and preferences; understanding these can significantly impact the effectiveness of marketing efforts. For instance, urban dwellers might prioritize convenience and environmental benefits, while suburban residents may focus on cost savings and reliability.

To create targeted campaigns, it is vital to segment the audience based on demographic factors such as age, location, income level, and lifestyle. Tailoring messages to address the specific concerns and interests of each segment can make marketing efforts more engaging and effective. For example, younger audiences might be drawn to the environmental advantages of rail travel, whereas older passengers could appreciate the comfort and reduced stress compared to driving.

Furthermore, using various media channels appropriate for each demographic ensures the message reaches the intended audience. Social media platforms like Instagram or TikTok can effectively engage younger generations, while traditional media such as newspapers and television might better serve older adults. Advertising on public transportation or at train stations also targets potential rail users directly.

Engagement through Storytelling

Stories are powerful tools to connect with people on an emotional level, enhancing the public perception of passenger rail. Narratives can illustrate personal experiences, highlighting the benefits of rail travel through relatable anecdotes. For example, sharing stories of daily commuters who save time and money or families enjoying scenic train journeys can evoke positive emotions and generate interest in rail services.

Incorporating diverse voices in these stories ensures a wider appeal. Highlighting testimonials from various demographic groups, such as students, professionals, retirees, and tourists, can showcase the broad applicability and benefits of rail travel. Additionally, featuring stories from those who've experienced significant improvements in their quality of life due to rail access can be particularly compelling.

Visual storytelling is another effective method. Using videos and images to convey real-life rail experiences can create a vivid, memorable impression. Short documentary-style clips showing the journey of a particular commuter or a timelapse video of a scenic route can captivate audiences and reinforce the positive aspects of rail travel.

Strategic Partnerships

Collaborating with organizations that support sustainable transport initiatives can amplify promotional messages and foster greater acceptance. Partnerships with environmental groups, urban planning associations, and local government bodies can lend credibility and broaden the reach of advocacy efforts.

Partnering with environmental organizations, for instance, can help emphasize the eco-friendly aspects of rail travel. Joint campaigns focusing on reducing carbon footprints and easing traffic congestion can resonate well with eco-conscious citizens. These partnerships can also provide access to additional resources, data, and platforms for disseminating information.

Similarly, working with urban planning and development bodies can highlight how passenger rail integrates into broader city planning efforts to create sustainable, livable cities. Demonstrating the role of rail in achieving goals such as reducing urban sprawl, improving air quality, and enhancing public spaces can garner support from policy makers and urban planners.

Business partnerships can also be explored. Collaborating with companies that prioritize corporate social responsibility (CSR) can lead to joint promotions that underscore mutual benefits. For example, businesses might offer incentives for employees who commute by rail, thereby promoting rail use while showcasing their commitment to sustainability.

Utilizing Data-Driven Messaging

Finally, presenting clear, backed-up information is crucial in challenging misconceptions and promoting accurate facts about passenger rail. Misconceptions about the cost, efficiency, and safety of rail travel often hinder its acceptance. Counteracting these myths with concrete evidence can shift public opinion favorably.

Market research and data analytics play a pivotal role in crafting factual and persuasive messages. By analyzing usage patterns, satisfaction surveys, and economic impact studies, advocates can present compelling arguments supported by hard data. For example, showcasing statistics on reduced travel times, lower commuting costs, and decreased greenhouse gas emissions can make a strong case for rail adoption.

Transparency in communication is equally important. Detailed explanations of funding, construction timelines, and anticipated disruptions during project implementation can build trust. Sharing success stories and case studies from other regions where rail systems have been effectively integrated can also inspire confidence.

Educational campaigns are needed to inform the public about the long-term benefits of rail investments. Workshops, webinars, and informational sessions can be organized to engage community members and provide a platform for addressing questions and concerns. Additionally, using infographics and interactive online tools can simplify complex information, making it accessible and understandable.

The Role of Media in Shaping Opinions

Media representation and coverage play a pivotal role in shaping public opinion, especially regarding passenger rail services. Understanding how these portrayals influence perceptions is a crucial step in developing strategies to promote rail initiatives more effectively. Media can either build positive narratives around passenger rail or perpetuate negative stereotypes, affecting public acceptance and support for such projects.

To begin with, analyzing media portrayals of passenger rail services reveals much about current public perceptions and the underlying narratives that need addressing. For instance, reports focusing on delays, accidents, or financial losses might contribute to a negative outlook. Conversely, stories emphasizing the convenience, safety, and environmental benefits can foster a positive image. By systematically monitoring and evaluating media content related to passenger rail, stakeholders can identify prevalent themes and trends. This analysis provides essential insights into which aspects require immediate attention and helps craft messages that resonate with public sentiment.

Building strong relationships with local media outlets is another effective strategy to ensure better coverage of passenger rail initiatives. Local journalists often have significant influence over community perceptions and can be allies in highlighting the benefits of passenger rail systems. Establishing trust and maintaining regular communication with these media professionals can result in more balanced and supportive reporting. Hosting press conferences, offering exclusive interviews, and providing detailed briefings on rail projects can help journalists report accurately and positively. Additionally, inviting media representatives to experience rail services firsthand can provide them with richer, more comprehensive perspectives, making their coverage more authentic and impactful.

In today's digital age, social media platforms offer an unprecedented opportunity to directly engage with audiences and shape public opinion. Utilizing social media strategically allows rail proponents to counteract negative perceptions and promote positive narratives. Social media channels provide a platform for real-time interaction where questions, concerns, and misconceptions can be addressed promptly. Regular updates about rail projects, success stories, and interactive content like videos and infographics can keep followers informed and engaged. Encouraging public participation through polls, Q&A sessions, and sharing personal stories of rail users can humanize the initiative and build a robust online community of supporters.

Moreover, launching comprehensive media campaigns that utilize various forms of media can significantly elevate public understanding and appreciation of passenger rail services. These campaigns can span across print, broadcast, and digital platforms, each tailored to its audience's unique characteristics. For instance, visually engaging advertisements showing the advantages of rail travel during peak traffic hours can capture the attention of daily commuters. Similarly, environmentally focused pieces on news websites can appeal to eco-conscious readers, while storytelling through short documentaries on television can reach a broader audience. Diverse media forms ensure that the message reaches different demographic segments, enhancing overall effectiveness.

An integrated approach combining traditional media, local journalism, and social media ensures a multifaceted outreach strategy, maximizing impact. Television and radio ads might target older demographics, while social media campaigns reach younger audiences. Collaborative efforts with influential bloggers and social media personalities can further broaden the campaign's reach, leveraging their established followings.

Guidelines for developing media relations are crucial in facilitating effective communication with local journalists. Firstly, it's essential to understand the interests and specialties of different media outlets to tailor pitches accordingly. Secondly, building rapport through consistent engagement and transparency establishes trust and reliability. Lastly, being proactive in providing timely updates and responding to inquiries fosters ongoing interest and commitment from the media.

Similarly, when harnessing social media platforms, certain guidelines ensure more effective engagement. Creating a dedicated team to manage social media accounts ensures consistent and coherent messaging. Using analytics tools helps track engagement rates and refine strategies based on performance metrics. Moreover, adopting a responsive approach by addressing comments and messages swiftly builds trust and credibility with the audience.

Conducting awareness campaigns also demands structured guidelines for optimal results. Clear objectives need to be defined, outlining what the campaign aims to achieve. Identifying target audiences ensures messages are tailored appropriately. Collaborating with creative agencies can help design compelling content suitable for various media formats. Measurement and evaluation mechanisms should be established to assess the campaign's impact and make necessary adjustments.

In essence, understanding how media representation influences public perception of passenger rail services lays the groundwork for strategic interventions. Building strong relations with local media, leveraging social media platforms, and launching targeted campaigns are all vital components of a successful strategy to overcome societal resistance. Through thoughtful analysis, proactive engagement, and diverse outreach methods, it is possible to reshape public narratives and foster a more favorable environment for passenger rail initiatives.

Concluding Thoughts

This chapter has identified various societal barriers to passenger rail adoption and explored strategies to overcome them. By emphasizing the convenience, cost-effectiveness, and environmental benefits of rail travel, a more favorable public perception can be cultivated. Tailoring communication to different demographics ensures that messages resonate with specific groups, building widespread support. Additionally, showcasing successful rail systems from other countries provides concrete examples of the advantages rail travel can bring.

Engaging local communities through events and collaborations with educational institutions helps normalize rail travel and integrate it into everyday conversations. Involving community members in decision-making processes fosters a sense of ownership and inclusion, making the initiatives more relatable and accepted. Consistent communication from transportation authorities maintains transparency and trust, further reinforcing public support. With these strategies, societal resistance can be reduced, paving the way for a future where passenger rail is a valued and integral part of our transportation system.

Chapter Fourteen

Regional and Local Initiatives

R egional and local initiatives play a crucial role in enhancing passenger rail services across the United States. This chapter delves into various state-funded projects and regional efforts that aim to improve connectivity, stimulate local economies, and provide sustainable transportation alternatives. By examining these initiatives, we can gain insights into how individual states and regions overcome unique challenges to bolster their rail infrastructure. These localized efforts often employ creative funding models and collaborative approaches, showcasing the potential for smaller-scale projects to make a significant impact.

In this chapter, readers will explore state-level rail projects, such as those in California and Virginia, which highlight successful public-private partnerships and innovative funding mechanisms. We will also look at inter-city rail connections like

Amtrak Cascades that bring economic benefits through enhanced regional mobility. Light rail and commuter trains in urban settings, exemplified by Portland's MAX Light Rail and Denver's RTD expansion, demonstrate the importance of integrated transit systems. Finally, the chapter will address the integration of rail services with other public transport modes and unique solutions tailored to different regions. Through these examples, the chapter aims to illustrate the diverse strategies and successes of regional and local initiatives in revitalizing America's passenger rail system.

State-level rail projects

State-funded passenger rail projects serve as significant pillars in enhancing regional transportation needs, showcasing the importance of creative funding models and localized efforts. One of the key approaches employed by states involves public-private partnerships (PPPs). These collaborations between governmental entities and private sector companies leverage resources and expertise to develop rail infrastructure efficiently. For instance, PPPs can draw on private investment to supplement public funds, ensuring that projects have adequate financial backing. This model not only eases the burden on state budgets but also accelerates project timelines as private firms often bring technological innovations and streamlined management practices.

Local tax supplements also play a crucial role in funding state-level rail initiatives. By leveraging local taxes, regions can secure consistent revenue streams dedicated to rail improvements. An example is the establishment of special taxing districts where property owners within a certain radius of a new rail line pay additional taxes. These funds directly contribute to the construction and maintenance of rail infrastructure, transforming the areas into well-connected hubs. Additionally, these tax increments are often justified by the promise of higher property values and improved community services stemming from enhanced rail connectivity.

The economic impact of state-funded rail projects extends far beyond the initial construction phase. State-level projects can stimulate local economies by creating jobs, both during the construction period and through the ongoing operation and maintenance of rail systems. The influx of jobs spans various sectors, including engineering, construction, and service industries, contributing to substantial employment opportunities within the region.

Increased tourism is another economic benefit, with improved rail services making it easier for tourists to travel within and between regions. Convenient and efficient rail connections encourage longer stays and more frequent trips, injecting vital revenue into the local hospitality and retail sectors. Furthermore, the presence of a reliable rail system can significantly increase property values in nearby areas. Improved accessibility typically leads to higher demand for housing and commercial spaces, benefiting property owners and local governments alike through increased tax revenues.

California and Virginia offer exemplary cases of successful state-led rail initiatives. In California, the Capitol Corridor and San Joaquin routes demonstrate how targeted state investments can rejuvenate regional rail services. The Capitol Corridor, connecting Sacramento and San Jose, utilizes state funds to maintain and improve rail infrastructure, resulting in one of the most reliable and frequently used routes in the state. Similarly, the San Joaquin route has seen increased ridership due to state-supported upgrades and expansions, improving connectivity in California's Central Valley.

Virginia's approach also underscores the potential of state involvement in rail projects. The Virginia Railway Express (VRE) operates commuter services in Northern Virginia, easing traffic congestion and providing a sustainable alternative for daily commuters. Virginia's multimodal strategy integrates rail with other forms of public transport, ensuring seamless transitions for passengers. State funding has been critical in maintaining and expanding VRE services, highlighting the state's commitment to enhancing regional mobility.

Despite the successes, these projects are not without challenges. Bureaucratic red tape remains a significant hurdle in many state-funded rail initiatives. The approval process for rail projects often involves multiple layers of government oversight, which can cause delays and inflate costs. Streamlining bureaucratic procedures is essential to ensure timely project execution. Additionally, balancing community input with technical requirements presents its own set of difficulties. Community engagement is vital for garnering public support and ensuring that the rail projects address the needs of local residents. However, technical specifications and safety standards must also be met, sometimes leading to friction between community desires and technical feasibility.

For example, proposed rail lines may face opposition from local communities concerned about noise, environmental impact, or changes to neighborhood character. Effective communication and collaboration with stakeholders can mitigate these issues, ensuring that community concerns are addressed while maintaining the technical integrity of the project. This balance is crucial for the long-term success and acceptance of state-funded rail initiatives.

Peter Wretzky

Inter-city rail connections

Connecting cities through improved rail service has the potential to significantly foster regional economic integration. Regional initiatives, often overlooked, can play a vital role in revitalizing America's passenger rail system.

A prime example of a successful intercity rail system in the U.S. is Amtrak Cascades, which operates in the Pacific Northwest between Eugene, Oregon and Vancouver, British Columbia. This route exemplifies how coordinated efforts across state lines can enhance both connectivity and convenience for passengers. The Cascades line not only supports local commuters but also attracts tourists, contributing to the overall economic health of the regions it serves.

The impact of improved inter-city connections on regional mobility cannot be overstated. Enhanced rail services broaden job opportunities by allowing people to commute more efficiently between cities. Economic growth follows as businesses gain access to a larger talent pool and new markets. For instance, improved rail services can make it feasible for someone living in Portland to work in Seattle, thus benefiting both cities. Additionally, these connections encourage tourism, boost retail and hospitality industries, and even increase property values near train stations.

However, advancing inter-city rail systems isn't without its challenges. One major obstacle is the competing interests among cities, each vying for limited resources and prioritizing their own needs. Coordination between different jurisdictions can become a political tug-of-war, complicating project implementation. Funding bottlenecks also pose a significant challenge. Securing continuous financial support from federal, state, and local governments is arduous, often leading to delays or scaled-back projects.

Despite these hurdles, potential innovations are on the horizon that can bolster the viability of regional rail initiatives. Smart ticketing systems, for example, offer a streamlined and modern approach to fare collection, providing convenience to passengers and reducing operational costs. These systems utilize digital platforms that allow seamless payments across different modes of transportation, enhancing the overall travel experience. Predictive analytics represents another exciting innovation. By analyzing data such as ridership patterns, weather conditions, and maintenance needs, predictive analytics can help optimize schedules, improve reliability, and reduce downtime.

Integrating these technologies requires initial investments, yet the long-term benefits could justify the costs. In particular, smart ticketing could address the issue of interoperability between different regional transport systems, simplifying transitions for passengers who may need to switch from rail to bus or other means of transport. Likewise, predictive analytics could preemptively identify and mitigate issues before they disrupt service, ensuring a smoother, more reliable journey for all.

Light rail and commuter trains

In the bustling urban landscapes of America, light rail and commuter train networks have emerged as vital components of the public transportation ecosystem. These systems not only provide an alternative to road travel but also contribute significantly to the overall sustainability and efficiency of city transit. A closer look at successful implementations of light rail systems, such as Portland's MAX Light Rail and Denver's RTD expansion, provides valuable insights into their role in enhancing urban mobility.

Portland's MAX Light Rail serves as a prime example of an effective light rail network that has transformed the city's transportation dynamics. Established in 1986, the Metropolitan Area Express (MAX) now spans over 60 miles with five distinct lines connecting various parts of the city and its suburbs. This extensive network facilitates convenient travel for residents and visitors, reducing reliance on personal vehicles. The MAX Light Rail integrates seamlessly with the city's bus services, promoting multi-modal transport options and making it easier for commuters to switch between different types of public transit. Additionally, MAX's development was supported by local initiatives and federal grants, demonstrating how collaborative funding efforts can lead to substantial improvements in urban mobility.

Similarly, Denver's expansion of its Regional Transportation District (RTD) highlights the transformative impact of light rail systems. By prioritizing connectivity and accessibility, Denver has successfully expanded its light rail from a modest beginning to a network covering nearly 80 miles. The introduction of new lines and extension of existing ones have not only improved access to downtown areas but also connected outlying neighborhoods, fostering greater economic activity and community development. Denver's focus on integrating land use planning with transportation projects underscores the importance of holistic urban planning in achieving sustainable growth.

Commuter trains also play a crucial role in alleviating highway congestion and supporting urban sustainability. These trains are designed to move people efficiently between suburban areas and city centers, thereby reducing the number of cars on the road and decreasing traffic jams during peak hours. For instance, the Metra system in Chicago exemplifies the benefits of commuter rail services.

With eleven lines radiating out from the city center, Metra provides a reliable and punctual means of transportation for thousands of daily commuters. This not only helps to reduce the environmental footprint associated with car travel but also enhances the quality of life by easing the stress of commuting.

In addition to their environmental benefits, commuter trains are integral to comprehensive urban planning strategies aimed at promoting sustainable development. Cities that invest in robust commuter rail networks often see parallel investments in related infrastructure, such as bike-sharing programs, pedestrian-friendly pathways, and eco-friendly bus fleets. These integrated approaches create a cohesive transit environment where different modes of transportation complement each other, offering residents multiple options for getting around. Furthermore, effective urban planning ensures that commuter train stations are strategically located near residential and commercial hubs, maximizing convenience and ridership.

Understanding the funding mechanisms behind these transport solutions is essential for replicating their success in other regions. Grants and tax incentives are commonly employed to support the development and expansion of light rail and commuter train networks. Federal and state grants provide initial capital for large-scale infrastructure projects, while local governments often implement tax increment financing (TIF) to generate revenue for ongoing maintenance and operations. Public-private partnerships (PPPs) also play a significant role, bringing together government resources and private investment to share risks and rewards.

One notable example of innovative funding is the "Build America Bureau," which offers low-interest loans and credit assistance for transportation projects. By providing access to affordable financing, this initiative has enabled several cities to launch or expand their rail services without imposing excessive financial burdens on taxpayers. Additionally, tax incentives such as property tax abatements or sales tax exemptions can attract private developers to invest in transit-oriented developments (TODs) near rail stations, further stimulating economic growth and increasing ridership.

However, despite the numerous advantages and funding opportunities, the development and expansion of light rail and commuter train networks are not without challenges. Community pushback is a significant hurdle that planners must navigate. Residents may express concerns about noise pollution, property devaluation, and changes to neighborhood character. Engaging the community through transparent communication and public consultations can help address these issues, ensuring that projects move forward with public support.

Regulatory compliance is another critical challenge. Navigating the complex web of federal, state, and local regulations requires meticulous planning and coordination. Environmental impact assessments, zoning laws, and safety standards must all be adhered to, often leading to delays and increased project costs. To mitigate these challenges, project managers must work closely with regulatory bodies from the outset, incorporating their requirements into the planning process to avoid costly revisions later.

Integration with other public transport modes

Integrating passenger rail services with other forms of transportation is a crucial step towards creating a seamless travel experience for commuters. This approach not only enhances convenience but also encourages the use of public transit, thereby reducing traffic congestion and environmental impact. One effective strategy to achieve this integration is through the synchronization of schedules between rail services and other modes of transport such as buses, metros, and bikes.

For instance, aligning the arrival and departure times of trains with local bus services can minimize waiting times for passengers and make transfers smoother. Similarly, coordinated schedules between trains and metro systems can ensure that passengers do not have to wait long periods for their next mode of transport. This level of synchronization requires meticulous planning and collaboration among various transport agencies, but the benefits are substantial. Commuters could enjoy shorter overall travel times, leading to increased satisfaction and higher ridership rates.

Seamless travel experiences also rely on cohesive planning to maximize public benefit and reduce environmental impact. Integrating passenger rail with other transportation options involves careful consideration of how these systems interact within the urban fabric. Planners must think about the location of train stations in relation to bus stops, metro entrances, and bike-sharing docks. The goal is to create a network that is easy to navigate, thus encouraging more people to leave their cars at home.

Cohesive planning also helps in designing ticketing systems that are user-friendly. A singular fare structure that works across different modes of transport can simplify the process for passengers. Instead of purchasing separate tickets for each leg of their journey, commuters could use a unified card or mobile app, making the transition between different transport modes as straightforward as possible. Such an integrated system not only improves the user experience but also facilitates data collection on travel patterns, which can inform better planning decisions in the future.

Despite these advantages, there are significant obstacles to achieving this level of integration. Conflicting interests among various transport agencies can pose a challenge. Each agency may have its own priorities and operational constraints, making it difficult to align goals and strategies. For example, a bus operator might prioritize routes based on local demand, whereas a railway company might focus on long-distance connectivity. These differing objectives can lead to a lack of coordination, ultimately hampering efforts to create a seamless travel experience.

Another major hurdle is the standardization of fare structures. Different pricing models and ticketing systems can complicate the integration process. For instance, a regional rail service might use distance-based fares, while a city bus network could charge flat rates. Harmonizing these fare structures requires negotiation and compromise, as well as investments in new technologies to support unified ticketing systems. Failure to address these issues can result in confusing and cumbersome experiences for passengers.

However, there are successful case studies that provide valuable insights into overcoming these challenges. San Francisco's Bay Area Rapid Transit (BART) system is a prime example of effective integration. BART connects with multiple forms of transportation, including buses, ferries, and bike-sharing programs, offering a cohesive travel experience for commuters. The introduction of the Clipper Card, a single payment method usable across different transit services, has streamlined the process for passengers, making it easier for them to switch between modes of transportation without hassle.

The success of BART highlights the importance of clear communication and collaboration among various stakeholders. Regular meetings and joint planning sessions can help align objectives and streamline operations. In addition, leveraging technology plays a crucial role in facilitating integration. Advanced software solutions can synchronize schedules in real-time, adjust for delays, and provide passengers with up-to-date information about their journeys.

Moreover, BART's emphasis on station design has further contributed to its success. By ensuring that its stations are strategically located near bus stops, metro entrances, and even bike racks, BART makes it convenient for passengers to transfer between different forms of transport. This kind of thoughtful infrastructure planning is essential for creating a seamless travel experience.

Peter Wretzky

Unique solutions for different regions

Adapting rail services to regional contexts is essential for achieving optimal efficiency and passenger satisfaction. Each region in the United States presents unique challenges and opportunities that must be addressed through tailored solutions. For instance, regions with higher population densities require different approaches than areas with dispersed populations. Geographic constraints such as mountainous terrains or coastal areas can also demand specific adaptations. These considerations ensure that rail systems are not only functional but also beneficial to the communities they serve.

Florida's Brightline and Minnesota's Northstar Line provide excellent examples of how regional characteristics shape rail solutions. Brightline, operating between Miami and West Palm Beach, caters to a densely populated area with heavy tourist traffic. Its high-speed trains offer frequent service, appealing to both residents and visitors looking for efficient travel options. On the other hand, the Northstar Line in Minnesota serves a more dispersed suburban population, connecting Minneapolis to its northern suburbs. This commuter line focuses on integrating with local bus services to extend its reach within the community.

Incorporating local culture into rail services can significantly enhance passenger experience and boost ridership. A rail system that reflects the identity and traditions of its region can foster a sense of pride and ownership among residents. For example, incorporating local art and design elements into station architecture, offering regional food and drink options on board, and hosting events or exhibitions that celebrate local heritage can all contribute to a richer travel experience. When passengers feel a connection to the rail system, they are more likely to use it regularly, thereby supporting its sustainability and growth.

Regional innovation initiatives are crucial in developing customized solutions for rail services. One such initiative is the implementation of on-demand systems, which allow passengers to schedule trips according to their convenience rather than adhering to fixed timetables. This flexibility can be particularly beneficial in less densely populated areas where traditional rail schedules might not be practical. Digital platforms also play a significant role in modernizing rail services. Mobile apps that provide real-time updates, ticketing options, and customer support can greatly enhance the user experience. Additionally, these platforms enable better data collection and analysis, allowing operators to continually improve services based on passenger feedback and usage patterns.

Investing in these innovations requires collaboration between various stakeholders, including government bodies, private companies, and local communities. Public-private partnerships can be an effective way to fund and implement new technologies and services. By sharing resources and expertise, these collaborations can drive progress and ensure that initiatives are well-aligned with regional needs and goals.

Customization of rail services also involves addressing economic factors. Affordability plays a key role in attracting riders, especially in areas with lower income levels. Offering tiered pricing models or discounts for frequent travelers can make rail travel more accessible. In addition, providing amenities that cater to different segments of the population, such as quiet cars for business travelers or family-friendly facilities, can broaden the appeal of rail services.

Environmental considerations are another important aspect of regional customization. Rail systems have the potential to reduce carbon emissions by offering a greener alternative to car travel. To maximize this benefit, it's essential to design routes and schedules that encourage high utilization rates. Using renewable energy sources to power trains and implementing energy-efficient technologies can further enhance the environmental sustainability of rail services. These efforts align with broader regional and national goals to combat climate change and promote sustainable development.

The success of customized rail solutions depends on ongoing evaluation and adaptation. Regularly gathering and analyzing data on passenger behavior, satisfaction, and operational performance allows operators to identify areas for improvement and respond to changing needs. Engaging with the community through surveys, public meetings, and online platforms can provide valuable insights and foster a sense of involvement. Transparency in communication and decision-making helps build trust and ensures that rail services remain responsive to the communities they serve.

Final Thoughts

The chapter has shed light on smaller-scale and regional initiatives aimed at improving passenger rail services in America. Through state-funded projects, inter-city connections, and the integration of multiple transportation modes, localized efforts have shown that they can significantly contribute to the revitalization of the nation's rail system. Key examples such as California's Capitol Corridor, Virginia's Railway Express, and Amtrak Cascades in the Pacific Northwest illustrate how targeted investments and collaborative funding models can enhance connectivity, economic growth, and environmental sustainability.

These regional ventures face challenges, including bureaucratic obstacles and competing interests, yet promising innovations like smart ticketing systems and predictive analytics foster optimism for future development. Cities like Portland and Denver demonstrate successful approaches to integrating light rail and commuter train networks with urban planning strategies. By focusing on tailored solutions that address specific regional needs and incorporating local culture into rail services, these initiatives not only improve transportation options but also build stronger, more vibrant communities. Through continued investment and innovation, localized rail projects hold the potential to transform America's passenger rail landscape.

Chapter Fifteen

Lessons from Failed Projects

A nalyzing failed rail projects in America provides essential insights into the multifaceted challenges that such ambitious undertakings often face. From political roadblocks to financial mismanagement, these projects present a rich source of lessons that can guide future endeavors in passenger rail development. Understanding why these initiatives faltered helps to inform policymakers and planners about critical pitfalls to avoid, thereby increasing the likelihood of successful implementation in the future.

This chapter delves into specific case studies, such as the California High-Speed Rail project and Florida's high-speed rail initiatives, to highlight the various obstacles encountered. It examines the role of political dynamics, funding challenges, technological hurdles, and public opposition in derailing these projects. Additionally, it addresses issues of mismanagement and corruption, drawing on examples from across the country to illustrate their detrimental impact. By scrutinizing these elements, the chapter aims to provide a comprehensive understanding of past failures, offering valuable guidelines for future rail projects.

California High-Speed Rail Challenges

One of the most ambitious infrastructure projects in recent American history is the California High-Speed Rail project. Despite its grand vision, this project has faced numerous challenges that have significantly delayed its progress and increased its costs. By examining these challenges, we can extract valuable lessons for future rail initiatives.

Political roadblocks have been a significant hindrance to the California High-Speed Rail project. From its inception, the project has navigated a complex political landscape, contending with shifting legislative priorities and fluctuating support from various government levels. Political shifts have resulted in inconsistent funding and policy changes, further complicating the project's timeline. For example, initially robust support from both state and federal sources saw sudden reductions or reallocations as political administrations changed.

This inconsistency affected long-term planning and added layers of uncertainty, making it challenging to maintain momentum and stakeholder confidence. In addition to governmental hurdles, public opposition emerged as a notable political obstacle. Residents and interest groups have voiced concerns over environmental impacts, noise pollution, and land usage, leading to legal battles and additional delays.

Cost overruns and budget mismanagement have plagued the California High-Speed Rail project, severely impacting its feasibility. Initial cost estimates were overly optimistic, failing to account for various complexities and contingencies. As a result, the project's budget ballooned beyond initial projections, eroding trust among stakeholders and the public. Early estimates pegged the project's cost at around $33 billion, but subsequent evaluations saw those numbers double, sparking outrage and skepticism. Financial miscalculations, such as underestimating land acquisition costs and construction expenses, have compounded these issues. Cost overruns stemmed from several factors, including rising land values, unforeseen environmental remediation needs, and escalating labor and material costs. Moreover, budget mismanagement has led to periodic cash flow problems, stalling important phases of construction and exacerbating delays. These financial inconsistencies highlight the importance of realistic budgeting and transparent financial management in large-scale infrastructure projects.

Technological hurdles have also contributed to the struggles of the California High-Speed Rail project. Land acquisition, a crucial step in the process, proved more complex than anticipated. The need to navigate through densely populated urban areas and environmentally sensitive regions introduced unprecedented challenges. Additionally, acquiring land at reasonable prices while balancing the rights and concerns of property owners slowed progress considerably. Construction methods, too, presented their own set of complications. Techniques suitable for high-speed railways often required specialized knowledge and equipment not readily available or familiar within existing local frameworks. For instance, constructing tunnels through geologically unstable terrain or installing tracks suited for high-speed trains posed considerable engineering challenges. These technological hurdles were inadequately addressed in initial planning stages, leading to extended timelines and unplanned expenditures.

Public engagement and communication failures have further complicated the California High-Speed Rail project. Effective stakeholder outreach is critical in any large infrastructure initiative, yet this project suffered from gaps in communication. Inadequate communication strategies led to widespread misconceptions about the project's scope, benefits, and impacts. Many communities along the proposed routes felt left out of the conversation, fostering resistance and dissatisfaction. Misinformation spread, magnifying fears about eminent domain seizures, environmental destruction, and community disruption. A more inclusive approach to public engagement, involving regular updates, transparent decision-making processes, and active solicitation of community feedback, could have mitigated some of these issues. Properly engaging the public not only builds trust but also ensures that legitimate concerns are heard and addressed.

Guidelines for future projects must account for comprehensive public engagement strategies. Ensuring continuous and transparent communication should be a priority. Establishing dedicated communication teams tasked with maintaining open lines of dialogue between project planners and affected communities can foster better relationships and reduce resistance. Creating forums for public discussion, providing clear and accessible information about project developments, and addressing concerns promptly are essential steps in building public trust and support.

Florida's Failed Initiatives

Florida's ambitious high-speed rail projects have faced numerous obstacles, shedding light on essential lessons for future endeavors. A key learning point is the disparity between vision and execution. Ambitious plans often failed due to leadership changes and inconsistent project visions. Initial proposals for high-speed rail in Florida promised revolutionary transportation that would connect major cities swiftly and efficiently. However, as leadership changed hands, each new administration introduced alterations to the project's scope, design, or priorities. This inconsistency created confusion and caused significant delays. For instance, while one leader might prioritize speed and technological advancement, another might focus on cost-cutting measures, thereby diluting the original vision.

Moreover, the lack of a unified long-term strategy meant that different facets of the project worked at cross-purposes. Without a cohesive direction, resources could not be effectively allocated, resulting in mismanagement and inefficiency. Consequently, the ambitious vision was seldom realized in its entirety, leading to public disillusionment.

Funding challenges also played a pivotal role in Florida's failed high-speed rail attempts. Financial difficulties, particularly the heavy reliance on federal grants, proved to be a double-edged sword. Federal grants, which were supposed to provide the bulk of the funding, came with stringent conditions and approval processes. Any change in federal policy or economic downturn impacted the availability of these funds, leading to financial instability. For instance, during economic recessions, federal budgets tighten, and funding priorities shift away from high-cost projects like high-speed rail.

Additionally, relying heavily on a single source of funding exposed projects to high risks. Diversified funding models, incorporating state funds, private investments, and public-private partnerships, were inadequate or poorly structured. The absence of a robust financial mix led to severe cash flow problems. Future projects must ensure multiple, stable funding streams to mitigate such risks. Establishing a diversified funding approach can buffer against unpredictable economic shifts and policy changes, ensuring that projects remain financially viable under varying circumstances.

Public sentiment and voter referendums significantly influenced the fate of these initiatives. Public opinion swayed the outcome of crucial funding measures through referendums, underscoring the importance of understanding and addressing local concerns. In several instances, Florida voters rejected funding initiatives necessary for advancing high-speed rail projects. These outcomes reflected deeper issues such as a lack of sufficient public engagement and education about the benefits of high-speed rail.

It's vital for future projects to engage communities early and often, fostering a sense of ownership and aligning the project's benefits with public interests.

Thorough outreach programs can help demystify the technical aspects of high-speed rail, making them more relatable and accessible to the general population. Furthermore, clear communication about the prospective economic, environmental, and social benefits, backed by case studies or evidence from regions where high-speed rail has succeeded, can build strong public support. Listening to and incorporating public feedback can turn potential opposition into advocacy, ensuring successful voter-backed initiatives.

Infrastructure gaps presented another formidable challenge. Florida's existing infrastructure was often incompatible with advanced high-speed rail systems, necessitating extensive and costly retrofitting. Urban areas, designed without considering future high-speed rail integration, required significant modifications. For example, the existing rail lines, road networks, and urban layouts did not align with the structural needs of high-speed trains, prompting expensive infrastructural overhauls. Additionally, retrofitting urban spaces to accommodate new rail systems often met with resistance from property owners, businesses, and local governments concerned about disruptions and relocations.

The costs associated with these modifications frequently exceeded initial projections, adding unforeseen financial burdens to the already strained budgets. Moreover, constructing new tracks through densely populated areas posed technical and logistical challenges, complicating project timelines and escalating costs. To address these challenges, future projects must incorporate thorough feasibility studies, realistic budget assessments, and phased implementation strategies. Integrating high-speed rail into existing urban planning frameworks from the outset can reduce incompatibilities, lower costs, and enhance project efficiency.

Mismanagement and Corruption Cases

In examining the realm of failed rail projects in America, one cannot ignore the profound impact that mismanagement and corruption have had on these initiatives. Through a close look at several case studies, we can understand how these detrimental factors have repeatedly undermined public trust and halted progress in passenger rail development.

The issue of corruption has been a recurring theme in many failed rail projects. Notable examples include the embezzlement of funds and fraudulent activities by officials involved in the administration of these projects. For instance, the infamous case of the North Carolina Railroad Expansion in the early 2000s revealed significant misappropriation of state funds. Senior officials were found guilty of diverting millions meant for the project into private accounts, severely damaging the project's credibility and causing long-term delays. Similarly, the Boston Big Dig project, although primarily a highway project, included rail components and was plagued by over $3 billion in cost overruns attributed to corruption and mismanagement. These cases highlight how ethical breaches not only cripple financial resources but also erode public confidence, making it challenging to garner support for future initiatives.

Beyond outright corruption, administrative inefficiencies play a critical role in the failure of rail projects. Poor management practices often result in a lack of accountability, leading to delays and budget overruns. For instance, the Chicago Transit Authority's (CTA) Red Line South Reconstruction project faced significant delays due to disorganized planning and poor coordination among the city's agencies. The lack of a coherent strategy led to frequent halts in construction and inflated costs. Bureaucratic red tape further exacerbated the problem, with multiple layers of approval processes slowing down decision-making and implementation. This underscores the need for streamlined operations and clear accountability structures within transit projects.

Transparency and accountability are vital mechanisms for mitigating the risks of corruption in rail projects. Enhanced oversight can play a pivotal role in ensuring that funds are appropriately utilized and that projects stay on track both financially and operationally. One successful example is the Washington Metro's Silver Line extension. After facing initial setbacks due to poor oversight and cost escalations, the project saw significant improvements through the establishment of an independent oversight board. This board was empowered to audit expenditures continually and ensure compliance with federal guidelines, leading to more efficient project management and restored public trust. Incorporating similar transparency protocols in future rail initiatives can greatly reduce the likelihood of mismanagement and foster a culture of integrity.

Guidelines for implementing effective oversight involve establishing independent audit bodies that regularly review project finances and procedures. Public disclosure of these audits ensures accountability and keeps stakeholders informed. Additionally, setting up hotlines and whistleblower protections encourages reporting of any unethical behavior without fear of retribution. Regular training programs for all personnel involved in the project on ethical standards and financial management can also help mitigate risks.

Recovery from past mismanagement offers valuable lessons on transforming failed projects into successful ventures. Several initiatives have managed to rebound by learning from their mistakes and implementing necessary reforms. The New York East Side Access project, which aimed to connect the Long Island Rail Road to Grand Central Terminal, initially suffered from severe mismanagement issues, including cost overruns and delays due to inefficiencies. However, a comprehensive overhaul of management practices, along with increased transparency measures, allowed the project to get back on track. By instituting regular performance reviews and holding contractors accountable for meeting deadlines, the project team could identify and rectify problem areas swiftly.

Successful recovery strategies often involve a thorough analysis of past failures to inform new approaches. For example, conducting post-project evaluations provides insights into what went wrong and how similar pitfalls can be avoided in the future. Implementing reforms based on these evaluations ensures that subsequent projects learn from previous errors, thereby improving overall project outcomes. Transparency in these efforts is crucial; openly communicating about the changes being made and the reasons behind them helps to rebuild stakeholder trust and increases public support.

One guideline for recovery includes developing a robust feedback mechanism that collects input from all stakeholders, including community members, policymakers, and contractors. This holistic approach ensures that diverse perspectives are considered in reform efforts. Continuous monitoring and adaptive management allow for real-time adjustments to project plans, reducing the likelihood of repeating past mistakes.

Public Opposition Case Studies

Public opposition has been a significant barrier to the success of rail initiatives in America. Understanding the dynamics and reasons behind this resistance is crucial for making future projects more successful. One notable example is the Peninsula Rail Program in California, where local communities organized resistance against the proposed high-speed rail connecting San Francisco to Los Angeles. Concerns ranged from environmental degradation to increased noise levels, leading to prolonged delays and inflated costs due to legal battles.

At the heart of these opposition movements lie genuine community concerns. Environmental worries frequently top the list, as citizens fear the potential destruction of natural habitats and the contamination of local ecosystems. For instance, in the case of the Denver FasTracks project, residents voiced their apprehensions about the adverse impact on air quality and green spaces. Noise pollution is another common theme; high-speed trains can significantly alter the acoustic environment of nearby neighborhoods. Residents living near rail lines often report stress and sleep disturbances due to constant train noise.

In addition to environmental and noise concerns, another factor that fuels public opposition is inadequate consultation with affected communities. When planning the now-defunct Texas TGV project, insufficient dialogue with local stakeholders led to a strong backlash. The lack of transparency and perceived disregard for citizen input fostered a sense of mistrust, compounding opposition efforts. It's clear that a failure to genuinely engage with the community can derail even the most well-intentioned projects.

Given these recurring themes, addressing community concerns effectively requires a multi-faceted approach. One effective strategy is negotiation and compromise. A prime example is the Sound Transit 3 project in Seattle, which successfully navigated public opposition through thoughtful engagement and willingness to adjust plans. By rerouting certain segments and incorporating additional noise-reduction measures, the project was able to move forward with broader public support. This demonstrates that accommodating community needs without sacrificing project goals is possible and beneficial.

Engaging detractors early in the planning process is another critical element of reducing opposition. Holding town hall meetings and workshops allows project planners to listen to community voices and integrate their feedback into the design. For instance, the extension of Boston's Green Line involved multiple rounds of public consultations, enabling planners to address concerns such as station locations and traffic disruptions. This proactive approach not only mitigated resistance but also fostered a sense of shared ownership among residents.

Communication strategies play a pivotal role in gaining public approval. Transparent communication builds trust and helps demystify the benefits of rail projects. An effective method is framing narratives in a way that highlights the long-term advantages of the project, such as reduced traffic congestion, lower carbon emissions, and improved public health outcomes. The New York State's Hudson Tunnel Project exemplifies this approach by consistently communicating its economic and environmental benefits through various media channels, helping to garner public and political support.

In promoting rail initiatives, social media proves to be an invaluable tool for reaching a broader audience. Campaigns can utilize platforms like Twitter and Facebook to engage with the community, share updates, and address misconceptions. Interactive Q&A sessions, live streams, and community polls are other ways to foster ongoing dialogue. The Miami-Dade SMART Plan successfully used these methods to keep the public informed and involved, leading to widespread local backing.

Gathering feedback via community forums ensures that public sentiment is continually gauged and addressed. Regularly scheduled forums provide a platform for residents to voice concerns, ask questions, and receive timely answers from authorities. This two-way communication helps maintain momentum and trust throughout the project's duration. The Los Angeles Metro Gold Line Extension used community forums effectively, ensuring continuous stakeholder engagement and promptly resolving issues before they escalated.

Adaptation of Failure into Learning Experiences

Analyzing failures provides crucial insights that can pave the way for future successes in passenger rail initiatives. By examining past mistakes, stakeholders can develop a comprehensive understanding of what went wrong and how to rectify those issues, potentially saving time, resources, and effort in future projects.

One of the most effective ways to learn from past project failures is through detailed case studies. These case studies not only highlight what went wrong but also showcase how other projects adapted post-failure by leveraging insights and restructuring efforts. For instance, the failed American passenger rail projects often draw parallels with setbacks in other industries, such as aerospace or telecommunications. By adopting best practices from these industries, rail projects can implement strategic changes that enhance their chances of success. The key here is to understand that failure is not an end but an opportunity to gather valuable lessons for future endeavors.

Moving forward, it is essential to discuss specific reforms catalyzed by past experiences. For example, after assessing various failed rail projects, policymakers have introduced stringent protocols for oversight and efficiency. These policy changes involve setting clearer goals, establishing transparent reporting mechanisms, and ensuring regular audits. A guideline in this context would be the establishment of dedicated committees tasked with monitoring every phase of the project, from inception to completion. These committees should include experts in transportation, finance, and urban planning to provide diverse perspectives and ensure thorough scrutiny.

A critical concept that underpins learning from failures is the implementation of cyclic learning and feedback loops. Continuous improvement necessitates conducting retrospective analyses where stakeholders review what worked and what did not.

This process encourages a culture of adaptation where teams are not afraid to pivot based on new information. For instance, after a project concludes, a debriefing session involving all key players can identify gaps and opportunities for improvement. Developing a guideline for these sessions is vital. Each meeting should generate actionable items, which are then tracked to ensure they are addressed in subsequent projects. Such iterative reviews help cultivate an environment where learning from past mistakes becomes second nature.

Failure often acts as a catalyst for innovation. Setbacks force teams to think outside the box, spurring creative approaches that may not have been considered otherwise. An example of this can be seen in how some projects have adopted cutting-edge technologies, such as advanced data analytics and AI, to streamline operations and predict potential bottlenecks before they occur. Encouraging an innovative mindset means creating spaces where new ideas can be tested without fear of failure. Living labs, for instance, can serve as experimental zones where novel concepts are piloted and refined. Fostering an innovative environment is about striking the right balance between risk-taking and strategic planning.

When reviewing case studies, several prominent examples stand out. Consider the redevelopment of the Northeast Corridor in the United States. Initially plagued by budget overruns and scheduling delays, the project underwent extensive restructuring. By incorporating lessons from previous missteps, including better stakeholder engagement and robust financial oversight, the initiative eventually set a benchmark for subsequent rail projects. Additionally, insights gained from the aviation industry's handling of complex logistics and safety standards were instrumental in refining operational procedures, underscoring the value of cross-industry learning.

To further illustrate the impact of thoughtful policy reform, one can look at the improvements in procurement processes. Historically, opaque procurement practices led to inefficiencies and cost overruns. Learning from these mistakes, recent reforms emphasize competitive bidding and clear contract stipulations. Establishing guidelines for procurement involves mandating transparency throughout the bidding process and ensuring that contracts include penalties for delays and deviations. This approach not only mitigates risks but also fosters a culture of accountability.

Feedback loops are particularly important in maintaining the adaptability of long-term projects. Setting up mechanisms for continuous monitoring and evaluation ensures that projects remain aligned with their objectives. A practical example of this is the introduction of performance dashboards, which track key metrics in real-time. Regularly updating these dashboards based on feedback enables timely interventions and course corrections. Guidelines for utilizing feedback loops should include periodic reviews, stakeholder consultations, and adaptive management strategies that allow for flexibility in project execution.

Innovation, sparked by failure, often leads to groundbreaking advancements. In the face of initial setbacks, some rail projects have turned to emerging technologies like blockchain to enhance transparency and efficiency. By decentralizing data and improving traceability, blockchain helps mitigate issues related to corruption and mismanagement. Such innovations are not confined to technology alone; they also encompass novel funding models, such as public-private partnerships (PPPs). These models distribute risks more equitably and attract private investment, thus reducing the financial burden on public coffers. To foster an innovative environment, project managers should create incubators where new ideas can be incubated and scaled.

Bringing It All Together

In this chapter, we delved into the challenges faced by various high-speed rail projects across America, focusing on the California High-Speed Rail as a primary example. Issues such as political roadblocks, cost overruns, technological hurdles, and public opposition have significantly hindered progress. By analyzing these setbacks, we have identified vital lessons for future initiatives, emphasizing the need for realistic budgeting, transparent financial management, effective public engagement, and adaptive planning.

These insights underline the importance of learning from past mistakes to inform future endeavors in passenger rail revival. A thorough understanding of previous missteps allows stakeholders to develop more robust strategies, fostering successful project implementation. As we move forward, embracing transparency, consistent funding models, and comprehensive public communication will be key to overcoming obstacles and achieving sustainable transportation goals.

Chapter Sixteen

Vision for the Future

B uilding a visionary roadmap for the future of American passenger rail is essential for transforming the nation's transportation landscape. As advancements in technology and growing environmental concerns make their mark, the time is ripe for America to reimagine its rail infrastructure. This chapter delves into the potential of creating a high-speed rail network that could revolutionize travel across the country. High-speed rail promises faster connections, reduced travel times, and a greener alternative to current transportation methods, sparking excitement among transportation enthusiasts, policymakers, and academics alike. The vision set forth highlights not just the benefits but also the practical steps necessary for making this ambitious project a reality.

In this chapter, readers will explore a detailed blueprint for establishing a high-speed rail system in the United States, drawing lessons from successful international models like Japan's Shinkansen and Europe's extensive networks. The discussion includes strategies for enhancing connectivity between major metropolitan areas and underserved regions, aiming to boost local economies and create jobs. Attention is given to investment priorities, detailing the need for modern signaling technology, new train sets, and overhauled maintenance facilities. Governance models are examined to illustrate how effective public-private partnerships and regional cooperation can streamline decision-making processes and funding efforts. Finally, the chapter underscores the importance of sustainability and public engagement, revealing how green practices and community input can shape a resilient and widely accepted rail system. Through these elements, this visionary yet realistic roadmap aims to lead America toward an innovative and sustainable transportation future.

Blueprint for a National High-Speed Rail Network

The vision for the future of American passenger rail includes a comprehensive framework for establishing a high-speed rail system. This system promises to transform transportation across the nation, bringing numerous benefits to various regions. High-speed rail can significantly improve connectivity between major metropolitan areas and underserved regions, providing faster, more efficient travel options for millions of Americans.

Major metropolitan corridors such as the Northeast Corridor, from Boston to Washington D.C., stand to benefit immensely from high-speed rail. These regions are densely populated with high levels of economic activity, making them ideal candidates for the introduction of high-speed rail services. Improved connectivity in these corridors could reduce travel times drastically, offering an attractive alternative to congested roads and crowded airports. Additionally, connecting cities like Los Angeles and San Francisco through high-speed rail could revolutionize travel within California, easing the strain on regional air traffic and providing a greener transportation option.

Underserved areas also have much to gain from the development of high-speed rail. These regions often lack robust transportation infrastructure, limiting economic opportunities and mobility for residents. By extending high-speed rail networks to these areas, it becomes possible to stimulate local economies, create jobs, and enhance access to larger markets and resources. For example, connecting rural regions in the Midwest to major urban centers can empower smaller communities and support more balanced economic growth nationwide.

Examining successful international high-speed rail systems provides valuable insights into how similar initiatives might be implemented in the U.S. Japan's

Shinkansen is a prime example of a highly efficient and reliable high-speed rail network. Since its inauguration in 1964, the Shinkansen has demonstrated remarkable safety records and punctuality, transporting millions of passengers annually with minimal delays. The technological advancements and operational excellence of the Shinkansen serve as a benchmark for what can be achieved with meticulous planning and investment.

Similarly, Europe's high-speed rail systems offer lessons in widespread adoption and integration. Countries like France, Germany, and Spain have developed extensive networks that connect not only major cities but also towns and villages across the continent. European high-speed rail systems have successfully combined speed with convenience, encouraging high ridership levels and reducing dependence on car and air travel. These international models emphasize the importance of strategic planning, government support, and public buy-in for successful high-speed rail implementation.

To establish a high-speed rail system in the U.S., it is essential to consider the necessary technologies and infrastructure adaptations. Safety and speed are paramount, requiring state-of-the-art signaling systems, advanced rail track designs, and cutting-edge train models capable of traveling at speeds exceeding 200 miles per hour. Incorporating future technological integrations, such as automated control systems and improved energy efficiency measures, will ensure that the rail network remains adaptable and sustainable in the long term.

Overhauling existing infrastructure to accommodate high-speed rail involves significant upgrades to tracks, bridges, and tunnels. Dedicated high-speed rail lines must be constructed to avoid conflicts with slower freight and commuter trains. Electrification of rail routes presents another crucial adaptation, facilitating faster and more environmentally friendly train operations. Investments in station modernization and accessibility are also critical to provide seamless travel experiences for all passengers, including those with disabilities.

Estimating the costs versus projected economic returns is a complex but vital aspect of planning for high-speed rail. Capital investment required for developing a high-speed rail network is substantial, covering expenses related to land acquisition, construction, technology procurement, and workforce training. However, the long-term economic benefits can outweigh these initial expenditures. High-speed rail can boost regional economies by attracting businesses, enhancing tourism, and fostering innovation clusters around key stations.

Operational costs, including maintenance and energy consumption, need careful consideration to ensure financial viability. High-speed railways typically benefit from economies of scale, where higher ridership levels can spread out operational expenses, making the service more affordable and sustainable. Public-private partnerships often play a crucial role in balancing funding needs, sharing risks, and leveraging private sector expertise to manage costs effectively.

Job creation is another significant economic advantage of high-speed rail development. The planning and construction phases alone can generate thousands of direct and indirect jobs across various sectors, from engineering and construction to manufacturing and logistics. Once operational, high-speed rail systems will require ongoing maintenance, operations staff, and administrative personnel, further contributing to employment opportunities.

Investment Priorities

Assessing the current state of infrastructure is crucial to revitalizing American passenger rail. The journey begins with a thorough evaluation of existing rail lines, bridges, tunnels, and stations. This assessment helps identify critical areas needing enhancement or replacement. Many parts of the rail network were built decades ago and have not kept pace with modern technological advancements. By pinpointing weak spots in the infrastructure, we can ensure the safety and efficiency of the entire system.

Peter Wretzky

One area requiring immediate attention is signaling technology. Modern signaling systems are paramount for maintaining safe and efficient train operations. Outdated systems can lead to delays, accidents, and inefficiencies. Investing in advanced signaling technology, such as Positive Train Control (PTC), which can automatically stop a train to prevent accidents, is essential for ensuring passenger safety and improving service reliability. Additionally, implementing real-time monitoring systems can enhance operational efficiency by allowing quick responses to any issues that arise on the network.

Safety upgrades are another critical focus area. Ensuring that all aspects of the rail system adhere to the highest safety standards minimizes risks and builds public trust in rail travel. Upgrading tracks, implementing advanced braking systems, and enhancing level crossing protections are vital measures. These improvements not only safeguard passengers and staff but also reduce the likelihood of costly disruptions and accidents.

In parallel with infrastructure assessments, investing in new train sets is indispensable. Modern, energy-efficient trains are at the heart of a sustainable future for passenger rail. Older trains tend to be less reliable, more expensive to maintain, and environmentally unfriendly. By procuring new train sets designed with the latest energy-efficient technologies, we can significantly reduce the carbon footprint of rail travel. High-speed trains, hybrid models, and electric multiple units (EMUs) are examples of this modern rolling stock that offers higher performance and lower environmental impact.

Maintenance facilities play a pivotal role in this investment strategy. A well-maintained train fleet ensures higher reliability and longer service life. Constructing state-of-the-art maintenance facilities equipped with advanced diagnostic and repair tools will streamline upkeep processes and reduce downtime. Regular maintenance schedules and refurbishment plans for older carriages further contribute to operational efficiency and sustainability.

Exploring innovative financing mechanisms is essential for actualizing these investments. Reliance solely on traditional funding sources may limit the scope and speed of rail development. Federal grants provide substantial support for large-scale projects but come with stringent requirements and competition for limited funds. State funds can complement federal assistance, contributing additional resources tailored to local needs and priorities. Public-private partnerships (PPPs) present a dynamic approach to financing, leveraging private investment for public infrastructure projects. PPPs can accelerate project timelines, distribute risk, and bring specialized expertise from the private sector, ultimately enhancing project outcomes.

Community-driven initiatives can also play a significant role in rail investment. Local communities have a vested interest in the success of their rail systems. Crowdfunding projects, local bond measures, and community investment trusts enable residents to directly support their transportation infrastructure. Engaging local stakeholders fosters a sense of ownership and commitment to the long-term well-being of the rail network.

Funding targeted pilot programs is another strategic approach to advancing rail revitalization. Pilot programs allow for the testing of new concepts and gathering data on their effectiveness before full-scale implementation. For example, a pilot program might test the viability of autonomous trains on a specific route, assessing their performance, safety, and public acceptance. Such pilots help mitigate risks associated with unproven technologies and provide valuable insights into their potential benefits and challenges.

Measuring the impact of these pilot programs is critical. Data collected during pilot phases can guide decision-making, highlighting successful strategies and areas needing adjustment. Public feedback is an indispensable component of this evaluation process. Engaging with passengers through surveys, community meetings, and online platforms provides insights into user experiences and preferences. Transparent communication about pilot program goals, progress, and outcomes builds public trust and supports informed dialogue about the future of rail investment.

Leveraging existing infrastructure is a cost-effective and pragmatic strategy. Many regions possess underutilized rail corridors and facilities that could be repurposed or upgraded to serve modern passenger needs. Revamping these assets reduces the need for extensive new construction and makes efficient use of available resources. For instance, converting freight rail lines to accommodate passenger trains can enhance connectivity without substantial new build-out costs.

Collaborative Governance Models

Effective governance structures are crucial for the successful implementation of a visionary passenger rail system in America. One key aspect is the role of public-private partnerships (PPPs). These collaborations can leverage private sector efficiency and innovation while utilizing public investment to minimize costs. For instance, the success of PPPs in Europe, such as the UK's Thameslink Programme, demonstrates how risk-sharing arrangements can lead to enhanced service quality and financial stability. The private sector's involvement often brings about improvements in technology and customer service, making the travel experience more pleasant and reliable. However, it is important to carefully design these partnerships to ensure that risks are balanced and that public interests are safeguarded.

Regional authorities play a critical role in addressing local needs and streamlining decision-making processes. Different regions have unique transportation requirements and challenges, which necessitate tailored governance models. For example, the Regional Transportation District (RTD) in Denver, Colorado, exemplifies an effective model. RTD coordinates various transit modes, from buses to light rail, ensuring seamless connectivity. By having a regional authority oversee the operations, there is a unified approach to planning and executing transit projects, reducing bureaucratic delays and fostering coherence with existing local transit systems. Furthermore, when regional authorities work closely with established transit agencies, they can harmonize schedules, fares, and services, creating a user-friendly network that encourages higher ridership.

Interagency cooperation across different levels of government is another vital component. Barriers such as fragmented responsibilities and funding challenges must be overcome to achieve cohesive policy-making and execution. A prime example is the collaboration seen in the Northeast Corridor

Commission, which involves state and federal agencies working together to improve the busiest passenger rail line in the United States. This cooperative model helps align policies, pool resources, and devise comprehensive strategies that address both immediate and long-term goals. Best practices from such models include establishing clear communication channels, setting shared objectives, and involving all relevant stakeholders from the outset. Effective interagency cooperation ensures that projects are well-coordinated, reducing redundant efforts and optimizing the use of available funds.

Community and stakeholder input are indispensable for the success and acceptance of any large-scale rail project. Engaging the public through feedback mechanisms and maintaining transparent communication can significantly enhance trust and support for the initiatives. Involving communities from the planning stages also helps in gathering diverse perspectives, ensuring that the projects meet the actual needs of the populations they serve. The California High-Speed Rail Authority's outreach program is a notable illustration of this approach. It includes frequent public meetings, online surveys, and forums where residents can voice their concerns and suggestions. This dialogue not only helps in refining project plans but also fosters a sense of ownership among the residents, making them active participants in the development process.

Peter Wretzky

Public-private partnerships are essential for modernizing the rail sector by bringing in much-needed capital and expertise from the private sector. They can help offset the financial burden on the government and inject innovative solutions into the project lifecycle. The Grand Paris Express project is one such example where a blend of public funding and private investment has led to the creation of an extensive metro network aimed at revitalizing the Greater Paris area. The project's governance structure balances public oversight with private sector efficiency, ensuring high standards in construction and operation. Nevertheless, it is crucial to establish clear contracts that outline roles, responsibilities, and performance metrics to protect public interests and maintain accountability.

Evaluating governance models of regional authorities is fundamental to tailor solutions that cater to specific local demands. In regions with dense urban populations, integrated transit systems overseen by a central authority can provide streamlined services. The Metropolitan Transit Authority (MTA) in New York City is an example of such governance. MTA oversees subways, buses, and commuter rail lines, providing a cohesive network that facilitates easy transfers and unified ticketing systems. Coordinating with existing transit authorities ensures that there is no duplication of efforts and resources are used effectively. Streamlined decision-making processes lead to quicker implementation of improvements and expansions, directly benefiting daily commuters and reducing road congestion.

Promoting interagency cooperation among different levels of government requires identifying and overcoming barriers that hinder collaborative efforts. One successful approach is the establishment of intergovernmental working groups focused on specific projects. The Gateway Program Development Corporation, responsible for the Gateway Tunnel Project between New York and New Jersey, illustrates how multi-level governance can function effectively. By bringing together federal, state, and local entities, the project benefits from a comprehensive strategy that addresses complex logistical, financial, and regulatory challenges. Such cooperation ensures that policies are aligned, and funding mechanisms are synchronized, maximizing the impact of each dollar spent and minimizing administrative hurdles.

Understanding the importance of community and stakeholder input cannot be overstated. Transparent communication and proactive engagement create an environment of inclusivity and responsiveness. Projects can benefit from local knowledge and gain social license to operate through genuine dialogue with affected communities. The Brightline rail service in Florida provides a case in point. Its developers engaged communities along the corridor through informational sessions, allowing residents to express their views and receive updates on progress. This two-way communication helped address concerns related to noise pollution, safety, and economic impact, leading to increased public support and smoother project execution.

Emphasis on Sustainable Practices

Integrating sustainable practices into the future of American passenger rail is essential for reducing the environmental footprint of transportation and fostering long-term ecological health. One critical area to focus on is the construction of stations and tracks. Sustainable building practices can include the use of eco-friendly materials that are sustainably sourced, such as recycled steel or renewable timber. Additionally, during construction, efforts must be made to minimize carbon emissions by employing energy-efficient machinery and optimizing logistics to reduce fuel consumption.

Another aspect is the sourcing of materials. Utilizing locally sourced materials can drastically cut down on transportation emissions, while ensuring these materials adhere to environmental standards helps promote broader sustainability goals. Construction companies should also implement waste reduction strategies, recycling materials whenever possible, and minimizing the overall impact of building activities on the surrounding environment.

Moving beyond construction, it's vital to evaluate opportunities for energy savings in rail operations. Transitioning to renewable energy sources such as solar, wind, or hydroelectric power can significantly lower the railway's carbon footprint. Rail operators could install solar panels on station roofs or along the tracks to harness natural energy. Additionally, innovative technologies like regenerative braking, which captures and reuses energy typically lost during braking, can further enhance energy efficiency.

Regenerative braking systems are already being utilized in some modern trains and have shown considerable promise in reducing energy consumption. These systems not only save energy but also contribute to overall operational cost reductions, making them a practical choice for sustainable rail systems.

Beyond energy considerations, promoting comprehensive multi-modal transportation networks is essential. This means creating seamless connections between different modes of transport, such as buses, subways, and bicycles, at train stations. Integrated transit systems make it easier for passengers to transition between different types of transportation, ultimately reducing reliance on personal vehicles and lowering overall emissions. For instance, bike-sharing programs at major train stations can encourage passengers to cycle to their final destination, contributing to healthier, more sustainable urban environments.

Synergies with biking and pedestrian initiatives can also be enhanced through thoughtful urban design. Developing dedicated bike lanes and pedestrian pathways that connect with rail stations ensures safe and convenient access for non-motorized travelers. This strategy not only reduces traffic congestion but also fosters a more active and healthy lifestyle among city dwellers.

Environmental restoration along rail corridors offers another vital approach to integrating sustainability. Proactive restoration projects can help rehabilitate degraded landscapes, enhance biodiversity, and create natural buffers that protect against soil erosion. By investing in green spaces linked to rail stations, rail companies can transform these areas into community hubs that offer recreational opportunities while supporting local ecosystems.

Community engagement plays a pivotal role in these sustainability efforts. Encouraging local communities to take part in environmental restoration projects can foster a sense of ownership and stewardship over these spaces. Educational initiatives and volunteer programs can empower residents to participate actively in maintaining green spaces, thereby strengthening the connection between the rail system and its surrounding environment.

Additionally, investments in green infrastructure can lead to lasting benefits for both the rail system and the community. Green roofs, rain gardens, and permeable pavements are examples of sustainable features that can be incorporated into station design. These elements not only manage stormwater effectively but also provide aesthetic value and enhance the urban landscape.

Incorporating public feedback into sustainability initiatives ensures that the needs and preferences of the community are considered. Through regular consultations, focus groups, and surveys, rail operators can gather valuable insights that inform the development and implementation of green projects. Transparent communication about ongoing and planned sustainability efforts builds public trust and encourages collective support for these initiatives.

Engagement and Education for the Public

Public engagement and education are critical components in fostering support for passenger rail initiatives. By informing and involving the public, these efforts create a more supportive environment for the development and implementation of rail projects. The benefits of rail travel must be communicated effectively to various demographics through targeted campaigns. These strategies can include social media outreach, community workshops, public service announcements, and collaborations with local media.

Raising awareness about the benefits of rail travel involves addressing different demographics through tailored messages. For younger audiences, environmental sustainability and the future benefits of rail travel are key points. For older generations, highlighting the convenience and safety of passenger rail may resonate more. Diverse messaging ensures that all demographic groups understand the value of investing in rail infrastructure. Additionally, visual storytelling through videos and infographics can make the information accessible and engaging.

Crafting educational initiatives around rail history and sustainability helps instill an appreciation for passenger rail among the public. Schools and universities play a pivotal role in this by integrating rail-related content into their curricula. Historical documentaries, interactive museums, and field trips can enhance students' understanding of rail travel's past and its potential future. Sustainability workshops can educate both young and adult audiences on how rail travel reduces carbon footprints compared to other modes of transportation.

Partnerships with educational institutions extend the reach of these initiatives. Universities can offer courses focused on transportation, urban planning, and environmental science that include modules on passenger rail systems. Interactive programs such as virtual reality experiences of rail journeys or model train building can engage younger students while teaching them about the technical and historical aspects of rail travel.

Establishing platforms for community input and feedback is crucial for maintaining public trust and gathering valuable insights. Town hall meetings, online surveys, and focus groups provide avenues for the public to voice their opinions and concerns. This feedback loop ensures that project planners are aware of community needs and preferences, leading to more effective and accepted rail initiatives. Transparency in project updates builds credibility and keeps the community informed about progress and challenges. Regular newsletters, dedicated websites, and social media updates can serve this purpose well.

Proactive communication is another essential strategy in public engagement. Anticipating community questions and concerns allows for better-prepared responses. Frequently asked questions (FAQs) sections on project websites, hotlines for immediate inquiries, and informational pamphlets distributed in high-traffic areas ensure that accurate information is readily available. Engaging with the community early and often helps mitigate resistance and fosters a sense of ownership among residents.

Harnessing local groups in advocacy can significantly amplify support for passenger rail initiatives. Local rail advocates bring a personal touch to broader campaigns, making the message more relatable. Empowering these advocates through training sessions, providing them with informational materials, and involving them in campaign planning ensures they are effective in their roles. Highlighting successful grassroots advocacy examples can inspire other communities to take similar actions, creating a ripple effect of support.

Encouraging coalitions between stakeholders adds another layer of strength to advocacy efforts. When local governments, businesses, and community organizations work together, their combined influence can drive policy changes and secure funding for rail projects. Collaborative events like stakeholder roundtables and joint press releases can demonstrate a unified front in support of passenger rail investments.

It's also important to showcase the positive impact of public engagement on past rail projects. Case studies from cities where public involvement played a significant role in the success of rail initiatives can serve as powerful examples. These stories can illustrate how community support helped overcome

challenges and led to thriving rail systems that
benefit everyone.

Summary and Reflections

The chapter has provided a comprehensive roadmap
for transforming American passenger rail through
high-speed networks, investment strategies,
governance models, and sustainable practices. It
explored how major metropolitan areas and
underserved regions can benefit from improved
connectivity, drawing on successful international
examples like Japan's Shinkansen and Europe's
extensive rail systems. The discussions also
emphasized the importance of modernizing
infrastructure through advanced signaling
technology, new train sets, and state-of-the-art
maintenance facilities.

In addition, the chapter highlighted the critical role of
collaborative governance, involving public-private
partnerships and regional authorities to streamline
decision-making processes. Community engagement
and stakeholder input were presented as vital
components for gaining public trust and support. The
focus on sustainability outlined ways to integrate eco-
friendly practices in construction and operations,
promoting renewable energy sources and multi-
modal transportation networks. Overall, the chapter

Peter Wretzky

illustrated a balanced and strategic approach to
revitalizing American passenger rail, aiming to create
an efficient, sustainable, and widely accepted
transportation system for the future.

Chapter Seventeen

Conclusion

In our journey through the pages of this book, we've explored the fascinating saga of American passenger railroads. From the golden age of rail travel to the hurdles faced in contemporary times, we have traced a path marked by continuous innovation, unexpected setbacks, and immense potential for revitalization. Understanding this evolution is crucial not only for transportation enthusiasts but also for policymakers, urban planners, and academic scholars who all play pivotal roles in shaping the future of sustainable transport systems.

One of our first stops on this historical ride was the era when passenger railroads were synonymous with luxury, efficiency, and connectivity. These iron horses symbolized progress and fostered economic growth, knitting together the fabric of American society from coast to coast. Yet, as we moved forward in time, the rise of automobiles and commercial airlines began to overshadow the glory days of rail travel. The advent of the Interstate Highway System and the ubiquity of air travel led to a significant decline in the use of passenger trains. However, this decline wasn't just about competition; it also highlighted critical gaps in policy and investment that allowed other modes of transportation to take precedence.

As we delved deeper into more recent history, we observed the persistent challenges facing American passenger railroads. Issues such as outdated infrastructure, underfunding, and a lack of coherent national strategy have all contributed to their struggles. Nevertheless, amidst these difficulties, there are glimmers of hope. Our examination revealed several resurgence efforts driven by dedicated advocacy groups, innovative transportation policies, and technological advancements. High-speed rail initiatives, for example, show promise in transforming regional connectivity and reducing carbon footprints.

In analyzing international case studies, we learned vital lessons about sustainable transportation and infrastructure improvements. Countries like Japan, with its exemplary Shinkansen, and European nations with their extensive network of high-speed trains, offer valuable insights. A common thread among these successful systems is sustained investment in infrastructure, coupled with robust public and political support. This lesson underscores the importance of viewing passenger rail not merely as a nostalgic remnant of the past but as a viable solution for contemporary and future transit needs.

Implementing these lessons requires a multifaceted approach. For policymakers and urban planners, the need for comprehensive planning and consistent funding cannot be overstated. Investment in modernizing rail infrastructure, enhancing safety measures, and integrating advanced technologies are imperative steps toward realizing a robust rail system. Moreover, fostering public buy-in through transparent communication and community involvement can help build the consensus needed to sustain long-term projects.

For the general public, there lies an opportunity to influence positive change through personal choices and collective advocacy. Whether it's choosing rail travel over less sustainable options or participating in local efforts to improve transit services, individual actions, when multiplied across communities, can create a significant impact. Imagine if every person reading this book advocated for enhanced rail services in their area—such collective efforts could generate a groundswell of support demanding a revitalized passenger rail network.

The concept of advocacy extends beyond mere support; it involves active participation in dialogues about transportation policies and sustainability initiatives. Attending public meetings, engaging with local and state representatives, and being informed about transportation issues are practical steps anyone can take to contribute to the cause. Public awareness campaigns highlighting the benefits of passenger rail —reduced traffic congestion, environmental sustainability, and economic growth—can further galvanize efforts at the grassroots level.

Envisioning a collaborative future for American passenger railroads allows us to dream of what can be achieved when policies, technologies, and public support align. Picture a national high-speed rail network seamlessly connecting major cities, where travel is swift, efficient, and environmentally friendly. Such a network would not only make rail travel a preferred choice for millions but also significantly cut down greenhouse gas emissions and reduce reliance on fossil fuels. Urban centers could see reduced congestion and pollution, while rural areas would benefit from increased accessibility and economic opportunities.

For urban planners and policymakers, this vision translates into action plans and strategic investments. It involves prioritizing rail projects in national agendas, exploring public-private partnerships to fund infrastructure development, and adopting innovative technologies to enhance efficiency and safety. The focus should be on creating an integrated transportation ecosystem where passenger rail complements other modes of transport, offering seamless, multimodal travel options.

For academic scholars and students, the future of passenger rail presents a fertile ground for research and innovation. Exploring new materials and technologies, studying the socio-economic impacts of rail investments, and developing models for efficient and sustainable rail operations are avenues that can drive progress. Academic institutions can collaborate with industry stakeholders to pilot pioneering projects, thus bridging the gap between theoretical research and practical application.

In conclusion, the story of American passenger railroads is far from over. It is a narrative rich with historical significance and brimming with future potential. By taking the lessons gleaned from both domestic experiences and international successes, we can chart a course toward a revitalized and sustainable rail system. This endeavor will require concerted efforts from all stakeholders—transportation enthusiasts, policymakers, urban planners, and the general public. Together, we can transform the vision of an efficient, interconnected rail network into reality, ushering in a new era of rail travel that honors its storied past while embracing the possibilities of tomorrow.

Chapter Eighteen

References

- https://hannawi.weebly.com/uploads/ 5/3/3/6/5336185/5.2.pdf

- https://oxfordre.com/americanhistory/display/ 10.1093/acrefore/9780199329175.001.0001/ acrefore-9780199329175-e-515? p=emailAmo1mmdmOxAmk&d=/10.1093/ acrefore/9780199329175.001.0001/ acrefore-9780199329175-e-515

- https://en.wikipedia.org/wiki/ History_of_rail_transportation_in_the_United_States

- https://www.encyclopedia.com/history/ encyclopedias-almanacs-transcripts-and-maps/ railroads-first-big-business

- https://www.strasburgrailroad.com/blog/10- railroad-tycoons/

- https://northeastmaglev.com/2018/10/09/the- golden-age-of-rail-in-the-usa-from-the-bo-to-the- transcontinental-railroad-to-the-northeast- maglev/

- https://www.reddit.com/r/MapPorn/comments/ 1do6gdg/ the_decline_of_passenger_railway_service_in_the/

- https://www.reddit.com/r/AskHistorians/ comments/23hrrl/ why_did_passenger_trains_die_out_in_the_us/

- https://history.howstuffworks.com/american-history/decline-of-railroads.htm

- https://www.reddit.com/r/urbanplanning/ comments/1dhi4z3/ what_caused_the_decline_of_forprofit_rail/

- https://northeastmaglev.com/2018/10/23/the-decline-of-the-american-passenger-railroad/

- https://www.everycrsreport.com/reports/ RL32709.html

- https://enotrans.org/article/amtrak-at-50-the-rail-passenger-service-act-of-1970/

- https://www.aar.org/wp-content/uploads/ 2020/07/AAR-Chronology-Americas-Freight-Railroads-Fact-Sheet.pdf

- https://www.cbo.gov/sites/default/files/108th-congress-2003-2004/reports/09-26-passengerrail.pdf

- https://www.jstor.org/stable/3325929

- https://www.downsizinggovernment.org/amtrak

- https://www.everycrsreport.com/reports/ RL32709.html

Peter Wretzky

- https://crsreports.congress.gov/product/pdf/R/R45942/7
- https://media.amtrak.com/2019/11/improved-safety-and-customer-experience-drive-record-amtrak-ridership/
- https://sgp.fas.org/crs/misc/R45942.pdf
- https://www.amtrak.com/content/dam/projects/dotcom/english/public/documents/corporate/businessplanning/Amtrak-Service-Line-Plans-FY21-25.pdf
- https://www.cato.org/cato-handbook-policymakers/cato-handbook-policymakers-9th-edition-2022/amtrak
- https://media.amtrak.com/wp-content/uploads/2021/05/Amtrak-2021-Corridor-Vision-May27_2021.pdf
- https://www.apta.com/wp-content/uploads/Speedlines_HSIPR_Issue_33_March2022.pdf
- https://s3.us-east-1.amazonaws.com/rpa-org/pdfs/2050-High-Speed-Rail-in-America.pdf
- https://www.masstransitmag.com/rail/article/55094403/new-report-outlines-ways-high-speed-rail-projects-can-be-completed-faster-in-us
- https://hsr.ca.gov/wp-content/uploads/2022/08/PB_01_PandN_Rev12_a11y.pdf
- https://www.apta.com/wp-content/uploads/Speedlines_HSIPR_Issue_37.pdf

- https://economie.esg.uqam.ca/wp-content/
  uploads/sites/54/2023/05/High-speed-rail-and-
  the-spatial-distribution-of-economic-
  activity-1.pdf

- https://insights.weareeverise.com/japan-
  blending-culture-and-innovation

- https://eeesa.com/en/bullet-train-japan/

- https://www.eesi.org/papers/view/fact-sheet-
  high-speed-rail-development-worldwide

- https://pure.iiasa.ac.at/1225/1/XB-80-508.pdf

- https://www.mdpi.com/2412-3811/6/5/68

- https://www.hsr.ca.gov/docs/about/
  business_plans/
  BPlan_2012InternationalCaseStudies.pdf

- https://www.cer.be/images/publications/essay-
  series/05_CER_ESSAY_FS.pdf

- https://www.itf-oecd.org/sites/default/files/
  docs/dp201330.pdf

- https://
  australasiantransportresearchforum.org.au/wp-
  content/uploads/2022/03/2013_henn_sloan.pdf

- https://op.europa.eu/webpub/eca/special-
  reports/high-speed-rail-19-2018/en/

- https://d-nb.info/1129406326/34

Peter Wretzky

- https://www.apta.com/wp-content/uploads/ Resources/resources/reportsandpublications/ Documents/greenhouse_brochure.pdf

- https://www.mdpi.com/2075-5309/14/2/539

- https://www.kcata.org/about_kcata/entries/ environmental_benefits_of_public_transit

- https://www.easemytrip.com/blog/why-are-trains-good-for-the-environment

- https://transportation.ucla.edu/blog/5-environmental-benefits-sustainable-transportation

- https://scholarsarchive.byu.edu/cgi/ viewcontent.cgi?article=1405&context=etd

- https://www.itf-oecd.org/sites/default/files/ docs/dp200816.pdf

- https://www.sciencedirect.com/science/article/ pii/S2773032822000050

- https://www.toolazytostudy.com/free-economics-essays-answers/benefits-of-investing-in-high-speed-rail

- https://www.railcan.ca/wp-content/uploads/ 2020/05/Moving-People-Products-and-the-Economy-the-Economic-footprint-of-Canadas-rail-industry.pdf

- https://www.linkedin.com/pulse/revolutionizing-transportation-impact-high-speed-rail-kalea-texeira-zauwe

- https://www.tandfonline.com/doi/full/ 10.1080/03081060.2020.1828935
- https://www.sciencedirect.com/science/article/ pii/S2214367X24001509
- https://blog.emb.global/impact-of-hyperloop-in-marketing/
- https://transportnextcon.com/the-future-of-transportation-hyperloop-and-maglev-trains/
- https://www.hsrail.org/blog/maglev-hyperloop/
- https://railroads.dot.gov/federal-state-partnership-intercity-passenger
- https://www.railcan.ca/wp-content/uploads/ 2023/02/A-Parliamentarians-Guide-to-Canadas-Railways.pdf
- https://tc.canada.ca/en/corporate-services/ transparency/briefing-documents-transport-canada/2023-dm/transport-canada-structure-portfolio/transport-canada-s-groups-regions/ policy
- https://canadagazette.gc.ca/rp-pr/ p2/2024/2024-07-03/html/sor-dors152-eng.html
- https://otc-cta.gc.ca/eng/publication/ departmental-plan-2024-2025
- https://tc.canada.ca/en/corporate-services/ transparency/corporate-management-reporting/ departmental-plans/transport-canada-2023-2024-departmental-plan

Peter Wretzky

- https://rosap.ntl.bts.gov/view/dot/60849/
  dot_60849_DS1.pdf

- https://www.sciencedirect.com/science/article/
  pii/S0003687023000686

- https://www.railfans.ca/advocacy-and-lobbying

- https://www.linkedin.com/pulse/revolutionizing-
  transportation-impact-high-speed-rail-kalea-
  texeira-zauwe

- http://www.ontario.ca/page/connecting-ggh-
  transportation-plan-greater-golden-horseshoe

- https://imfg.org/report/transportation/

- https://www.railwaygazette.com/us-government-
  allocates-82bn-to-inter-city-rail-initiatives/
  65501.article

- https://dot.ca.gov/-/media/dot-media/
  programs/rail-mass-transportation/documents/
  rail-plan/6-chapter-6csrpfinal.pdf

- https://www.sciencedirect.com/science/article/
  pii/S2667091723000031

- https://tc.canada.ca/en/corporate-services/
  transparency/corporate-management-reporting/
  transportation-canada-annual-reports/
  transportation-canada-2011/rail-transportation

- https://www.nytimes.com/2022/10/09/us/
  california-high-speed-rail-politics.html

- https://calmatters.org/economy/2023/03/
  california-high-speed-rail/

- https://transportation.house.gov/uploadedfiles/
  2023-11-29_mr._ohanian_-_testimony.pdf

- https://www.chapman.edu/wilkinson/_files/
  pdf%20white%20papers/dan-mcnichol.pdf

- https://www.vox.com/policy-and-politics/
  2019/2/15/18224717/california-high-speed-rail-
  canceled

- https://www.commerce.senate.gov/2024/5/
  congressional-gop-transportation-leaders-
  probing-failed-california-high-speed-rail-project